Photo Retouching
with
Adobe Photoshop

By Gwen Lute

Amherst Media, Inc. ■ Buffalo, New York

DEDICATION

If I dedicated this book to all the individuals that made it possible, there would be so many people involved it would require a whole new book to list everyone! There are a few specific individuals that I do want to recognize.

First: Thanks to an all-loving, all-knowing Being I refer to as my Source and my Light for the endless gift of enthusiasm and retouching skills with which I have been blessed.

Second: My brother in law, Ivan Travnicek, for giving me the initial idea and spending untold hours with me to put the first book together. Although this present book is wholly different, I feel he planted the idea seed. I also want to thank his wife, my sister Deani for keeping that seed watered, often sharing those long hours with us.

Third: I want to thank Craig Alesse and Amherst Media for having faith in this project, and their staff for working closely with me to make it happen.

Fourth: I must say the most important individual is my loving husband, Ronald K. Lute, who has been supportive from the beginning. As I began the project of this version of the book, he patiently (and sometimes not so patiently!) sat behind me spending endless hours as a scribe translating each move I made as I made it, writing it in such a way that other people can understand what I was desiring to convey.

Last but not least this book could not have been possible without the many photographers and individuals who agreed to allow their work and their images to be displayed in this book as demonstration projects. Every image used in this book was an actual job completed by me for a customer.

Copyright © 2000 by Gwen Lute

All rights reserved.
"Maximum Sized Prints from Various Digital Files" chart courtesy of Eastman Kodak Co., Inc.

Published by:
Amherst Media, Inc.
P.O. Box 586
Amherst, NY 14226
Fax: (716) 874-4508
Publisher: Craig Alesse

ISBN: 0-936262-91-5
Library of Congress Card Catalog Number: 98-74593

Printed in the United States of America
10 9 8 7 6 5 4 3 2 1

Table of Contents

Introduction

■ The Art of Retouching

In normal art forms the work of art is produced from scratch — on a blank canvas or from a lump of clay. The retouching artist begins with a completed but flawed product that needs repair. A good retoucher or restoration artist can complete a job so that the customer is unable to tell where corrections were made to the photograph. The final product should be better than the original. Cracks should disappear, and missing areas of the image should be restored. It is difficult and challenging.

Professional photographers of all kinds seek out independent retouchers and restoration artists as the photographer's expertise is photography, not the art of repairing an image. Portraits will need to have zits, crows feet, moles, scars, birthmarks, bruises, bald patches, glare and blemishes of all types removed. You may even be asked to move heads around, or to take individuals out of a picture. Friends and relatives who know a person well automatically edit out the various imperfections when they look at the person, but when they see an unretouched picture, they don't think the person looks natural. It is the retoucher's job to help people look their best!

Do not change the character of an individual or an animal without permission of your customer. All professional photographs are copyrighted. The copyright privilege will seldom, if ever, belong to the retoucher no matter how much work goes into repairing the image. The retoucher should have the permission of the photographer before making any changes to a professional photograph. A photographer will usually provide the retoucher with a complete list of retouching instructions, and sometimes a proof print with instructions marked on the print.

The ethics of retouching become the most tenuous in dealing with real events. A retoucher must be careful not to be drawn into illegal activity, such as manipulating a picture for a court case or an insurance settlement. In an accident picture, don't move the wrecked cars around. If you are unwittingly duped, you won't be held liable, but it is best to stay on guard and not be drawn into anything that could be perceived as illegal.

By adhering to these simple cautions, you can experience the joys of restoring images without worry. Retouching and restoration is fun and soon you will not only be having great entertainment, but can be making good money as well. This book is designed to show you how.

"Professional photographers of all kinds seek out independent retouchers..."

■ A Historical Perspective

The art of photography began in the 1800's with black and white photography. Along with photographs came the need to alter them or remove blemishes in the images. In the beginning portrait photo retouchers used a long sharpened shaft of graphite to retouch a negative. This practice continued for many decades. The etching knife was soon discovered as a useful adjunctive tool to create eyelashes and other dark aspects of the photographs.

Retouching was introduced shortly after the beginning of photography, but it took the glamour girls of Hollywood of the 1920s and 1930s to bring beauty to a high form of illusion. Airbrush artists have been used since the early 1930s, and demand for this service has been high. Airbrush artists create the polished-looking art used in advertising, publishing, movie posters and men's magazines, where goddesses are created out of mortal flesh.

Hand tinting soon became an art form. This process began with the use of dry powders on daguerreotype portraits, then made a transition to oil and watercolor paints with the debut of paper photographic processes. Color dyes have been readily used by photo retouchers to tint black and white photographs. The dyes are absorbed by the emulsion and become a natural and permanent part of the photograph. Color oils were used as an alternate means of colorizing as well; but, in contrast to dyes, they require extended drying time and well-ventilated work areas.

With the advent of color film came the need for color retouching methods. Dyes remained a primary retouching process, using a brush for application. A newer product provides dyes in individual pens. Pastels have become popular as well. The important consideration for the retoucher is to choose the most appropriate method for a particular project.

Most recently, companies, like Adobe, developed programs to fulfill digital retouching needs. Most texts and demonstrative software focused on creation of graphic arts, not retouching. The advent of digital retouching did not mean that traditional retouching became obsolete. Technically oriented individuals purchased photo retouching programs and attempted to compete in the retouching market by offering digital retouching as an option to traditional methods. They were capable of following technical processes, but often lacked the artistic skill and knowledge of the experienced retoucher. Seasoned retouching artists had no desire to abandon their learned tools.

One of the first barriers to using digital retouching is that the individual must learn a whole new language. Bits, Bytes, and Megabytes, not to mention RAM and ROM are but a few of the terms. All computers and equipment are not equal in value and usability. These barriers alone are enough to keep most retouchers from exploring the art of digital retouching.

"... companies, like Adobe, developed programs to fulfill digital retouching needs."

A photographer's camera falls apart during a wedding. The dark line that results would seem to equal disaster and possible legal action against the poor photographer. But with the assistance of digital retouching, not so!

■ Why Use Digital Retouching?

Long before I became involved with digital retouching, I worked as a retouching artist in my parent's color lab. I remember an instance where they were faced with a dilemma: Our photographer had taken a series of family portraits of a group of six sisters. All except the youngest sister looked beautiful in the best shot, but she had her head hanging down with eyes closed. The family did not like the portrait. The only picture available of her where she looked good was taken farther from the camera, everyone else looked bad, and her head was smaller than in the other image. All of the staff said it could not be corrected. I took it upon myself as a challenge, went into the darkroom and eight hours later (making many adjustments to the enlarger and using various printing techniques) produced an acceptable portrait. I can now easily complete this same task digitally in a few minutes.

There are many projects that the modern photographer encounters that can be dealt with more easily and quickly using digital techniques. Some projects are simply impossible with standard retouching techniques, have become possible through the use of computer retouching.

When the customer desires a number of prints, or even a number of prints of various sizes, it is better to reproduce from a negative. The reason for this is both quality and economics. The image is scanned, retouched one time, output to film, and printed. The end product may be expensive, but is less costly in the long run if multiple images are desired. The result will also be a high-quality print, even at large sizes. In contrast to a high resolution digitally produced negative, a hand-retouched negative may appear to be flawed. Major alterations to the picture (such as installing a better head on the body) were almost impossible in manually retouched negatives.

ADVANTAGES OF DIGITAL
> ADDING OR SUBTRACTING OBJECTS OR PEOPLE
> PROVIDE NEW AND/OR DIFFERENT BACKGROUNDS
> ARRANGING ITEMS IN AN IMAGE
> REPLACING MISSING PARTS
> COLORIZING
> REPAIR OLD, DAMAGED AND DESTROYED IMAGES
> REMOVE DISTRACTIONS

DISADVANTAGES OF DIGITAL
> REQUIRES INVESTMENT IN COMPUTERS AND SOFTWARE
> COST IS OFTEN PROHIBITIVE FOR MANY CUSTOMERS
> STANDARD COMPUTER MEMORY IS OFTEN INADEQUATE
>   TO RUN THE PROGRAMS

Old photos that are a part of a family's ancestral records may be presented to you for restoration. These family heirlooms may have cracks or other damage. In the past it would be almost impossible to restore these photos to their original state. With the assistance of digital retouching, the image can be completely restored by recapturing and reprinting it on new paper.

■ THE WAVE OF THE FUTURE

The future of the retouching industry lies in the area of digital retouching. Predictions by film producing companies is that film will become obsolete by the year 2010. While this may or may not happen, digital cameras are growing in popularity and availability as the cost moves into the reach of the consumer. It is only reasonable to be prepared and trained for this eventuality in the future.

■ RETOUCHING SOFTWARE

Photoshop is the software program for both the Macintosh and Windows-based computers. There may be many other photo retouching programs available for a lot less expense. But Adobe says it best in one of their advertisements: "Now you can do the impossible on a daily basis." The fact is no other program can currently compare with Photoshop. Many consider their products to be adjunctive to Photoshop because they cannot compete directly.

THE PHOTOSHOP ADVANTAGE

The latest upgrades of Photoshop consistently provide necessary changes that allow the Photoshop user to accomplish much more in a logical, efficient, and stable manner. Many improvements are implemented better than in any other program, allowing ease of use and versatility.

Photoshop has incorporated many positive features more recently. Some of the key additions are:

MULTIPLE UNDOS.
PHOTOSHOP IS CAPABLE OF TRACKING AS MANY AS 99 OPERATIONS, GIVING THE USER THE POSSIBILITY OF BACKTRACKING ONE OPERATION AT A TIME, OR REVERTING AT A MOUSE CLICK TO EARLIER STAGES OF CORRECTIONS.

MULTIPLE FILTERS.
THERE ARE MANY FILTERS AVAILABLE IN THIS PROGRAM. THE BASIC PURPOSE OF THESE FILTERS IS TO APPLY SPECIAL EFFECTS TO IMAGES. NOT ONLY ARE SPECIAL FILTERS AVAILABLE, YOU CAN ALSO CREATE YOUR OWN WITH THE ASSISTANCE OF THE PROGRAM.

EDITABLE TYPE.
ADDING TEXT TO A PHOTOGRAPH HAS NORMALLY REQUIRED ADDITIONAL SOFTWARE PROGRAMS. PHOTOSHOP INTRODUCED A FEATURE THAT ALLOWS YOU TO CREATE EDITABLE TYPE. TYPE REMAINS EDITABLE IN ITS OWN LAYER UNTIL YOU CHOOSE TO RENDER IT INTO PIXELS.

ACTIONS.
WHEN YOU ARE GOING TO BE COMPLETING A REPETITIOUS TASK ON MULTIPLE FUNCTIONS, THESE TASKS CAN BE SAVED AND USED AGAIN. A SIMPLE CLICK OF A BUTTON WILL PRODUCE THE SAME ACTION ONCE AGAIN AS NEEDED.

Consistent Color Management. Photoshop has been modified to maintain consistent color output when moving images to other systems. The bottom line is that you can get a consistent color match from what you see on screen to the output device.

■ Plug-Ins

Plug-ins are processing programs that enable new features. A number of importing/exporting automation and special effects plug-ins are included in the Photoshop program. The availability of additional plug-ins allows you to add optional functionality from third-party vendors.

1. GETTING EQUIPMENT IN ORDER

■ EQUIPMENT: NECESSARY

The first step in digital retouching is to ensure that the proper equipment is available to you. Just as with any important task, if you do not begin with the right tools it can be a pretty frustrating process. Keep in mind that the industry is producing bigger and better models of equipment all the time. It is up to you to research the latest technology, and to research current technology prior to making your investment.

■ THE COMPUTER

It does not matter whether you invest in a new computer or use the computer you already own — whether it is a Macintosh, Windows, or a Windows NT computer. The important thing is to be sure the computer meets the minimum power requirements. If you are choosing a Macintosh computer, it must be a Power Mac with a 7.5 or later operating system. If a windows compatible computer, it must have a pentium-class or faster processor with Windows 95 or later version, or a Windows NT 4.0 or later version.

■ RAM

With RAM (Random Access Memory), more is better. Either type of computer must have a minimum of 32 MB of RAM; 64 MB of RAM is highly recommended. The bottom line is, you need to equip your computer with as much RAM as you can. It is best to get RAM units after you purchase the computer and install them yourself. However, if you are new to the computer game and feel uneasy about doing this, you can purchase it already installed (but it'll cost you bunches more to do it that way). How much RAM is really enough? While Adobe recommends at least 64 MB, my feeling is that 80 MB is adequate, but limiting, especially with large files – these larger files will often end up crashing your computer. Go for 200 megabytes or more if you are working with a customer who requests film (a negative) as the end result.

■ HARD DRIVE

A minimum of 60 MB of available internal hard drive space is required to install and run Photoshop. Most modern computers are now being sold with gigabytes of hard drive (currently 2.5 and up). The internal hard drive on your computer should be at least 1 gigabyte in size. Larger is better! Computers also vary in speed. The speed is determined by a microprocessor. The faster the microprocessor oper-

"How much RAM is really enough?"

COMPUTER SHOPPING

The important thing to do when buying a new computer is to shop for the best deal you can get; while closeout models can be obtained at a large discount, keep in mind that you may not want to sacrifice reliability and warranty coverage for cost savings. Sometimes it pays to shop the local classified ads or to cruise the Internet for used equipment. Wherever you find your computer, make certain it meets the minimum standards and your needs for warranty coverage. The latest versions of Photoshop will not run without adequate power and memory! For example, if you are considering a Macintosh, Photoshop requires a minimum of a Power Mac.

ates, the less time it takes for you to progress from one phase of your task to the next. So, suffice it to say: Get a computer with the largest memory and hard drive and the fastest microprocessor you can afford!

■ KEYBOARD

Select a keyboard that feels good to you. It should feel comfortable when you are working since you may be spending extended hours at a time with it. There are a number of brands and prices ranging from about $30 to $170.

■ MOUSE

Most computers are normally sold with a mouse as standard equipment. If you must purchase a mouse, don't go cheap. Select a quality product that is going to provide you with a smooth operation, unless you are planning to primarily use an available alternative (see Equipment: Suggested).

■ CD-ROM DRIVE

Most newer models of computers come with a CD-ROM drive as part of the built-in internal drive equipment. Older models frequently do not have a built-in drive, and you must purchase and install the CD-ROM. Regardless of whether you have a CD-ROM as an internal or as an external drive, you must have one. Photoshop requires a CD-ROM to load and run the program. If you need to purchase a CR-ROM, a recordable CD-ROM (CD-R or CD-RW) might prove to be a good investment for the future as it adds the option of creating your own CDs for storage.

■ THE MONITOR

While some computers may come equipped with a monitor, they are usually 13" monitors. My recommendation is that you purchase a name-brand monitor that is at least 17", and capable of showing millions of colors. This may involve purchasing and installing a video card for your computer. The smaller the dot pitch rating of the monitor, the better. Do not get a 17-inch monitor with a dot pitch number greater than 0.28. A 20 or 21-inch monitor is better because the larger size monitors allow you to see the work you are doing more clearly.

■ EQUIPMENT: SUGGESTED

■ STORAGE DEVICES

In addition to the internal hard drive, you will need one or more removable storage devices that are widely compatible. These devices provide a storage module that allows you to record your finished work and transport or store it. Choosing a removable that is widely used is the safest course of action.

"Products offered by Iomega are very useful and are almost universally used by service bureaus."

Products offered by Iomega are very useful and are almost universally used by service bureaus. The Iomega Zip drive offers 100 megabytes of storage space, and is a reasonably inexpensive storage device. The Iomega Jaz drive is offered in 1 gigabyte or 2 gigabyte storage sizes. Syquest is another company with a strong line of products well entrenched in the graphics/service bureau industry. Syquest has a 1.5 gigabyte removable hard drive called the SyJet, and an EZFlyer drive that stores 230 megabytes.

A second alternative that is becoming increasingly popular is CD recordable drives. There are two options available: the CD-R drive (records only) and the CD-RW drive (rewritable). Obviously the better choice for a working storage unit would be the Rewritable CD which allows you to erase stored work on the CD and then re-write over it. RW disc media is more expensive, but RW drives will often accept either media. Both can be read by standard CD-ROM drives which makes them highly portable and compatible.

■ EXTERNAL HARD DRIVES

External hard drives are a means of significantly expanding your storage and work space. Models range from about 2.1 gigabytes to 18 gigabytes. Various models also have various speeds. The greater the storage space and speed, the greater the cost of these devices. While the external hard drive will free your internal hard drive space and make your work much easier, it does not take the place of a removable storage drive.

■ SCANNERS

A flatbed scanner is almost indispensible in doing the kind of work described in this book. A color scanner converts printed images into digital pictures. Scanners use colored filters or a prism to read RGB (red, green and blue) intensities, and then combine these three single color scans to provide a full-color image. These machines may take one or three passes to read the colors; they vary in bit depth (the amount of color information they capture at each reading) and in their resolution (how many readings per inch they take).

There are many scanner manufacturers, and like other fields in the computer industry, the technology is changing rapidly. It is important to review the latest computer magazines for articles that compare and rate scanners on the market. You should be most concerned with the scanner's faithfulness to colors and detail. The specifications of a scanner tell you how much data it captures, but not how accurate that data is. Image quality results vary from one scanner to another, even if they have the same ratings. The very minimum acceptable DPI rating for retouching is 400 x 400 optical DPI. Most flatbed scanners now are 600 x 1200 DPI or higher. Interpolated resolutions (another resolution often used by salespersons) will be higher, but less accurate. Base your decisions on optical DPI only. Make sure the scanner you are investing in has a sealed casing. Older models of scanners were designed with air vents in order to provide ventilation. The problem is that these vents also allow dust to flow into the scanner, and that can ultimately show up on your scanned images. A sealed scanner prevents this problem.

■ GRAPHICS TABLET

The graphics tablet comes with a pen that allows you greater freedom in your retouching process. It is best to try them out before purchasing one. The smaller sizes (e.g., a 6" x 9" size) are effective and more economical than the larger models.

■ TRACKBALL

Trackball technology is also rapidly changing. Basically, the trackball is a replacement device for the traditional mouse. The advantage to the trackball is that it allows the user to move the cursor with a stationary device. There are no frustrations associated with a mouse running off the edge of your mouse pad. More expensive models with larger balls generally offer more control of movement. Some models have additional button features which allow the user to customize specific functions.

GRAPHICS TABLET ADVANTAGE

While a graphics tablet is not a necessity, and you can easily use a mouse or a track ball with Photoshop, I feel once you have learned to effectively use the tablet you will not want to use anything else.

2. Capturing the Digital Image

■ The Difference in Color

Black and white photographs are perhaps the simplest form of prints to work with because they require less memory. Color prints become more complicated, and the problems compound. The task becomes simpler when you understand the basic concepts of color theory and processes, and how color prints differ from color transparencies.

■ A Color Primer

Basic photographic color images are created with dyes and pigmented colors. Final color is either directly applied, or colors are mixed to produce the result. For example, if you want green instead of yellow grass, you add a transparent wash of blue dye (yellow and blue mixed together form green). If you are retouching with dyes and you want to change something to black you would use a complimentary color. For example, if you want to correct the common photographic problem of red eye, a green dye would be used to turn the red to black. To correct blemishes on transparencies the same principle is used.

When scanning a color picture into your computer to use in Photoshop, you can work on the image in RGB or CMYK color. RGB (red, green and blue) takes up less image size space, and is normally the color mode required by color labs for photographic print and film output. Most print shops, service bureaus and some color labs work with CMYK (cyan, magenta, yellow and black). Complete the corrections in the RGB mode, and save the finished product in its final version in the CMYK mode for those processors that require CMYK. Check with your service provider for the required mode before beginning the job.

■ Scanning Techniques

The basic goal for beginning a retouching or a restoration process is to get the original print into your computer with photographic quality maintained. If you feel you can't afford to purchase a scanner, consider renting one by the hour. Many printing shops, for example, will rent you the complete realm of computer equipment, including the scanner, for an hourly rate. They will also provide you assistance with your job, but the rate can be very expensive. The other alternative is to have a service bureau do the scanning work for you.

A basic flatbed scanner will meet most of your input needs. Scan images at at least 300 DPI for reproduction at the same size. However, there are occasions when your scanning needs exceed the capabilities of your flatbed scanner. The primary concern involved in this process must always be achieving photographic quality. Often when a person

THE COLOR WE SEE

I had a wonderful experience many years ago when attending a Kodak retouching workshop. They demonstrated how a pure white light, when passed through a prism, breaks down into primary colors. When primary colored lights are combined together, they produce a pure white light. In order to see color, light must strike colored pigments, such as those in paints and dyes, and reflect back so we can see it. The combination of the color of light striking an object and that object's color make up the color we see.

"Before you scan the picture, wipe it with a non-lint cloth."

invests in a flatbed scanner, they think all of their problems are solved, but they may be wrong. For example, a picture destined for use as a poster, billboard or negative will require a very high resolution. To get this type of high-quality scan, you will need to obtain a drum scan. The price of a drum scanner is prohibitive for most individuals, so this is where your friendly service bureau comes into the picture. The cost of scanning through a service bureau will be much more economical than attempting to purchase a drum scanner for your personal use. You need to be sure and tell them the desired DPI and/or the final image size, the type of computer you are using, and the format you want the file saved in.

Before you scan the picture, wipe it with a non-lint cloth. Also, clean the glass platen on your scanner. Otherwise you will spend hours in Photoshop cleaning the dust spots off your image that could have been prevented in a couple of seconds by using a soft, lint-free cloth. When you are finished working with the picture and it is ready for processing, be sure to save it in the size the customer wants, otherwise the service bureau or color lab will charge you for the resizing service. Check with your lab for their requirements.

Work with the original print regardless of the print size, unless it is quite small. With a small picture, you may want to increase the scanned image size. Black and white pictures should be scanned as a grayscale image.

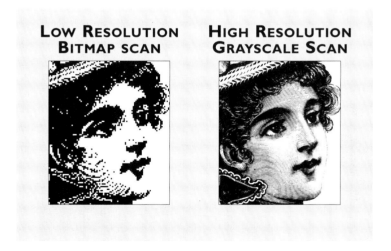

LOW RESOLUTION BITMAP SCAN   **HIGH RESOLUTION GRAYSCALE SCAN**

Now that you have your image scanned and converted from picture to digital image, you are ready to begin retouching or restoring the picture.

STEP 1:

Window
Hide Tools
Show Navigator
Show Info
Show Options
Show Color
Show Swatches
Show Brushes
Show Layers
Show Channels
Show Paths
Show History
Show Actions
✓ Illustration # 7 @ 33.3% (RGB)

3. RESTORING AN IMAGE

■ USING A LAYER AS A MASK

Our first project will involve removing an unwanted, distracting object from a picture, in this case a person standing behind a show dog. The owner of the dog would like to have this fine animal standing alone so she can be the center of interest in the picture to be used in a professional dog breeder's magazine.

Once the picture is scanned and in your computer as a digital file, you can accomplish the task readily and easily using layers as masks. This will become clearer to you if you want to experiment, or as you just follow along with the steps:

STEP 1:
Open the picture in Photoshop. If the Layers Palette is not already open on your screen, open it (Windows>Show Layers).

STEP 2:
Double click on the Lasso tool. The Lasso Options dialogue box will come up on your screen. Set the Feather Radius to 10. Select the desired area by click-dragging to the right of the Eucalyptus tree's trunk with the Lasso tool. The area being selected is defined by a dotted line. Select the whole leafy area. Hold the mouse button down until the whole area is outlined. To finalize your selection, release the mouse button.

THE LASSO TOOL

When working with the lasso tool, hold down the mouse button until the entire selection is outlined. If you take your finger off of the button before you return to the beginning point, the program will automatically join the lines from where you released the mouse button and where you began.

FEATHER RADIUS

Feather Radius can be used with all selection tools if you desire a soft edge on your image. For smaller size files you use smaller Feather Radius sizes. However, the smaller the radius setting, the harder the edges. Choose a larger number to provide a softer edge. Be aware that hard lines on the edge of the selection gives away the idea that the image has been altered.

STEP 4:

STEP 3:

Paste the selected area in a new layer on top of itself [Command/Control]+C (copy) [Command/ Control]+V (paste). You will notice that in the Layers Palette there is a Layer 1 which contains the area you just selected.

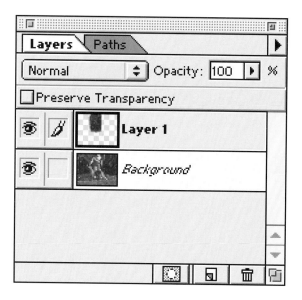

STEP 4:

Press the letter "V" or select the Move tool (top right tool in the tool box). Drag Layer 1 on top of the woman, above the dog. Don't be concerned if it covers part of the dog. The copied selection will not cover the complete image of the woman.

In order to cover her completely, you will need to make additional copies of Layer 1. Use as many duplicate layers as you need. The important task is to make certain she no longer shows in the picture. To duplicate Layer 1, click and drag Layer 1 down to the Create New Layer icon box at the bottom of the Layers Palette. The only part of the woman you will not want to cover up is the segments of the hand and forearm over the tree trunk.

STEP 5:

Select parts of the tree trunk, creating a new layer, and overlay the area to be deleted. Repeat this action until the forearm and hand are completely covered. Try not to create obvious patterns in the area that you are layering.

STEP 6:

With the woman's image above the dog covered, these layers are ready to be linked together. Select each layer in the Layers Palette except for the background layer (Last layer in the pallet list). Begin by clicking on the top layer to highlight it. A brush will appear next to the eye icon (second box from the left).

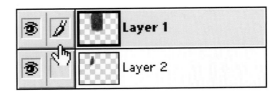

In other related layers, this box will be empty. Be sure you have clicked on the eye icon of the Background Layer to produce a blank box. Click on the black triangle in the upper right corner of the Layers Palette to display a pop-up menu. Click on Merge Visible, and release.

STEP 7:

Go to the Layers Palette, locate the Opacity window and enter "75." You will notice that the Eucalyptus layer over the woman becomes transparent. This creates a see-through mask that reveals the full image of the dog. The Lasso tool can be used to select and erase large general areas of the layer. Outline areas with the Lasso and press the Delete button. Make sure you don't go too close to the edge of the dog's image when doing this. Use the Eraser tool for the finer, close work. Use a large brush for the general area, and a smaller brush size for closer work. (Brush size can be changed by depressing the Bracket keys.) It is important that the erasures are precise, which may require the Zoom size to be increased at times.

STEP 8:

Go to the Window menu and click on it. Select Show Navigator. At the bottom of this palette, you will see miniature mountains with a slider in between them. Move the slider toward the big mountains to approximately 150% enlargement. Place the cursor (little white hand) in the Navigator tool box (red box), moving the box until the dog's head becomes centered in the original picture. Use the Eraser tool with both a small and a fine brush (as appropriate) to fine-tune your image to ensure the dog can be seen clearly beneath Layer 1. Once you are ready to continue, return to

BRUSHES

When using Brushes, the brush size can be adjusted by using the Bracket keys located to the right of the "P" key on the keyboard. Push the left bracket to reduce brush size, and the right bracket to increase brush size.

THE HISTORY PALETTE

The History palette records every click of the mouse, providing you a snapshot for each click. This is very good if you need to go back to undo or check previous work. However, this process takes up **RAM** space for each stored step. If you have completed a task, and won't need to check your work from that point backward, or you have limited **RAM** in your computer, it is important to purge the History palette periodically. To purge the pallet, go to the Edit menu and select **Purge All (Edit>Purge>All)** and click **OK**.

STEP 10:

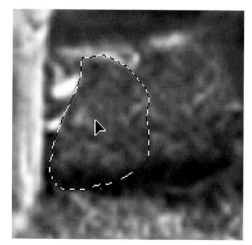

the Navigator tool box, move the slider to the left toward the small mountains until you once again can see the whole picture.

STEP 9:

Return the Layers Palette Opacity setting back to "100." Once again, check the image to ensure no part of the Eucalyptus tree layer's mask remains on top of the dog. If there is, go back and remove it until the dog stands free of the Eucalyptus branches. Problems may appear as a "cloudy area" on the dog's fur. Do a final check by going to the Layers Palette, then click the eye icon of the Background Layer to turn it off.

This will show if any obvious parts of the layer remain on the dog. These areas can be deleted with the aid of the Lasso or the Eraser tool. This work must be precise.

STEP 10:

Now we are ready to move to the Background Layer. Click on the eye first. Then highlight the Background Layer by clicking on it, and zoom into the area containing the woman's legs and shadow. Press the letter "L" to bring up the Lasso tool. Draw a small circle around a grassy area, hold down the [Command/Control]+[Option/Alt] keys. You will notice a black and white arrow. This allows you to duplicate any selection without having to copy and paste into a layer. This process can be repeated, and you just continue to pick up that same segment of grass. Drag and drop these grassy areas over any areas containing the woman's legs and shadow. Fine tune your work by using the Rubber Stamp tool.

RUBBER STAMP CAUTION:

Do not create obvious patterns in the area that you are changing. These will call attention to your alterations!

STEP 11:

Set the Painting Cursors to Brush Size and Precise (File>Preferences>Displays).

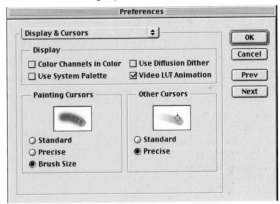

STEP 12:

Double click on the Rubber Stamp tool in the tool box. Go to the Rubber Stamp Options dialogue box and select Normal from the pop-up menu next to the Opacity setting. Next set the Opacity at 100%, select Aligned, and under Stylus select Size and Opacity (if not already selected).

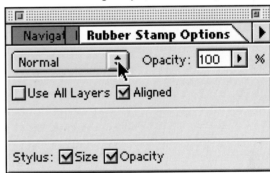

STEP 13:

Hold down the [Option/Alt] key and click on the grassy area next to the woman's shadow. Release both the [Option/Alt] key and the mouse button. You will then see a white round circle and a white cross hair displayed on the screen. Move the circle over the woman's shadow. It is better to use up and down movements to change the grass patterns, avoiding circular motions. [Option/Alt] click in varying areas to modify the grass patterns even more. Clean up any other extraneous areas, including any blue that might show through from the lady's blue jeans around the dog, and the leash hanging from the dog's neck.

BEFORE PRINTING!

The image must always be flattened before it is printed by a lab or service bureau.

LAYER OPACITY AND MODES

A.

B.

STEP 14:

The final step is to flatten the image. Go to the Layers Palette and click on the black triangle at the top of the palette. Select Flatten Image from the pop-up menu. This will combine all layers into one as the Background Layer.

■ LAYER OPACITY AND MODES

In this part we will consider how to use various Layer modes. We will begin with a wedding photograph that came out with a heavy black line covering the bride.

Illustration A (see sidebar) is a good image of the bride and B is the image we want to repair. Both Photos would obviously be scanned and saved prior to beginning this process. Note that the second image of the bride is larger than the first image that is being modified. This is something that can be altered during the restoration process.

STEP 1:

Open both images in Photoshop. Position and size the images so they can both be seen on screen.

STEP 2:

Use the Marquee tool to select the bride in Illustration A.

STEP 3:

Press "V" or select the Move tool. Place the Cursor in the middle of the Marquee in Illustration A and hold the mouse button down. Drag-drop the selection into Illustration B. The bride now stands facing herself in the image (and in a new layer).

STEP 4:

Flip the bride horizontally (Edit Menu>Transform> Flip Horizontal).

SAVING MEMORY

Purging can help free up memory for Photoshop and might keep you from running out of memory. It means to throw away a record of something Photoshop is retaining in memory. I like to purge the Clipboard often. To purge, go to the Edit menu and choose select Purge All (Edit>Purge> All) and click OK. This will purge Undo, Clipboard, Pattern and Histories. You can purge selectively by choosing individual items from the list.

STEP 6:

STEP 5:

Lower the Opacity of the upper layer to 65% so you can see through it. [Command/Control]+T will open the Transform tool. Click-drag the top left handle while holding down the Shift key at the same time (this scales the image proportionally as it is moved). Align the top (secondary) image over the original image (i.e., lining up the bodice). The Arrow keys can be used to move the image one pixel at a time. When the secondary image is placed appropriately, press Enter.

STEP 6:

Preserve as much of the original image as available by erasing parts of Layer 1. Use the Lasso tool with a Feather Radius of 20, draw a line around parts to be deleted, and push the Delete key. Since the bride's arm was intact in the original image, delete the arm on the secondary image.

STEP 7:

Return the Opacity to 100%, then clean up the final image using the various tools and methods for fine-tuning (i.e., the Rubber Stamp tool, the Eraser tool, the Lasso tool). You can see the final image below.

Notice that half of the groom's face is obscured.

C.

A second example that I feel is a simple but exciting demonstration of a combination of the use of both Layer Opacity and Layer Transformation involves removing the bride's veil from covering the groom's face in Illustration C (see sidebar). This could be a common problem that prevents an otherwise beautiful wedding shot from being acceptable.

STEP 1:

First, scan your picture into Photoshop.

STEP 2:

Using the Lasso tool with a Feather Radius of 5, draw a line around the visible cheek, lip, and inner edge of the eye areas.

STEP 3:

[Command/Control]+C, then [Command/Control] +V, will copy and paste to a new layer. Set the Opacity Slider in the Layer's palette to 68.

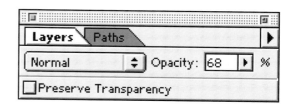

STEP 4:

STEP 4:

Flip the layer (Edit>Transform>Flip Horizontal). Place the Cursor outside the box at the upper right corner of the box, and the Rotation Arrow will appear. Rotate box counter-clockwise until eye and ear are aligned. The sides of the face do not match perfectly. Use the [Command/Control] key to distort the layer. Use the handles to distort the groom's face to make it fatter, and to line up the ears. When you have the face the way you think it should be, increase the Opacity to 100. Use the Arrow Keys to move the layer into place to finalize alignment.

STEP 5:

Remove the moles on the left side of the groom's chin by using the Lasso tool. Draw a small circle on the chin next to the area where the moles are using the Lasso tool. Click and drag holding the [Command/Control]+[Option/Alt] keys and drop the selection over the moles.

STEP 6:

Circle a swatch of hair just above the veil with an elliptical shape using the Lasso tool. Copy-paste to form Layer 2.

STEP 9:

SETTING OPACITY

When setting the Opacity you can easily do this by using the Number Keys, each number correlates to a percentage x 10 – i.e., 1 = 10%, 2 = 20%, etc.)

STEP 12:

STEP 7:

Select the Move tool and drag Layer 2 forming a natural hair line. Duplicate Layer 2 two more times, and move the duplicates into place.

STEP 8:

Merge Visible (as in the previous example) to join the three layers (Layer 2 and its two duplicates).

STEP 9:

Now we need to align the layered hairline until it blends in naturally with the hairline on Layer 1. Use Transform to line up the hairline lines approximately.

STEP 10:

Click on the Background Layer. Double-click the Rubber Stamp tool. Set the Opacity to 50%.

STEP 11:

Clean up all remaining remnants of the veil. This process will take you a little time to complete so it appears to hang naturally without covering any part of the groom's face. The tux may shine through rather than appearing as a dark area under the veil. If so, you may need to return to Layer 2 and use the Eraser tool to make the tux appear as a dark area.

STEP 12:

Create a new Layer. This new layer will be used to create a new veil along the remaining edge where the old veil was removed. Select the veil at right with the Lasso and align it with the hanging part of the veil. Copy, Paste and Transform. If you select undesirable parts that do not fit right, simply erase the undesirable part of the Layer.

Step 8:

Create Layer 4 by using the Lasso tool to copy the groom's ear. Make sure the ear is properly placed, using whatever alignment techniques that may be required. To make sure the ear is properly lined up, go to the tool box and open the Ruler. Anchor one end on the top of the stable ear, and the other end on the top of the replacement ear. Be sure the line runs right on top of the eyelids. It will once again appear as if the veil is over the groom's ear. Set the Opacity to about 40% (using your own judgment on this setting to create a realistic effect). Now Flatten the Image.

To complete the finishing touches for this image we will need to use Dodging and Burning Techniques which are discussed in the next section.

"Be sure the line runs right on top of the eyelids."

■ LAYERED DODGING AND BURNING TECHNIQUES

The processes of Dodging and Burning are professional dark room expressions for techniques to darken or lighten parts of the image. These techniques may be used when a person wants to create either a shadow or a highlight on the final image.

In a darkroom Dodging is done by holding an instrument between the light and the paper to block the exposure. Burning is the opposite, allowing light to strike for a longer exposure in an area of the image.

The Photoshop icon for the Dodging tool resembles a paddle, and the one for Burning resembles a curled hand. These tools tend to create a harsh effect. Layers will be used to soften the effect in the following example. We will continue working with the image of the bride and groom.

STEP 1:

Step 1:

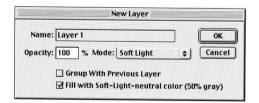

Step 1:

Go to the Layers palette and hold down the [Option/Alt] key while clicking on the Duplicate Layer icon at the bottom of the palette. This will open a New Layer dialogue box. Select the Soft Light mode and the option for Fill with Soft-Light-neutral color (50% grey) will appear. Check the box and click OK. Photoshop will create a new layer filled with 50% gray.

Step 2:

Open the Swatches palette (Windows>Show Swatches).

STEP 2:

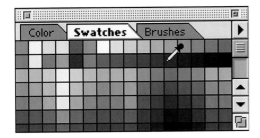

STEP 6:

The top two rows of the Swatches palette are Gradient Shades of Gray.

STEP 3:

Choose a Dark Gray in the middle of the second row by clicking on it. Select the Air Brush tool in the tool box and press [2] (the keyboard shortcut for 20% in the Airbrush Options box). Make sure the Normal setting is selected. Paint the areas under the groom's chin and on the ear to create a realistic shadow. Highlights on both the bride's and groom's faces can also be toned down.

STEP 4:

To bring a twinkle into the eyes of both the bride and groom, use the Airbrush tool. From the color Swatches select the purest white available on the top row. Open the Brushes pallet and choose the smallest brush on the top row. Zoom in to the groom's eye area before you begin painting. Begin painting where there is a glimmer of highlight in the groom's eyes. When you are finished with the groom's eyes, work up the highlight in the bride's eyes.

STEP 5:

To tone down the shadow area behind the groom, return to the Brushes palette and choose a Soft Brush. Make the brush diameter approximately the same size as the width of the shadow area. Set the Zoom at 150% and begin painting the shadow behind the groom on the left side of the image. A smaller size Soft brush can be used to do the finer work.

STEP 6:

When all Dodging and Burning is complete, it is time to flatten the image. [Command/Control]+E will complete the merge.

While the example in this section was a relatively simple one, the techniques you have learned can be applied in many situations. We will revisit these techniques when we consider the process of illuminating shadows in a later section.

■ USING THE CHANNELS PALETTE

Images have one channel per color. Four color (CMYK) and three color (RGB) are color images, while in black and white pictures you have only a single channel, black. Using the Channels, colors can be readily separated out.

Bad bruises from a fall provide a challenging job for a retoucher.

D.

We will be using a CMYK image in the next example (see Illustration D). It provides a challenging job for the retoucher. What we want to accomplish first is to isolate the black in this image.

STEP 1:

Open the Channels Menu (Windows>Show Channels).

STEP 2:

Move your cursor to the Black Channel (Bottom of the Channels palette) and click on it. This shows you the grayscale information in the image.

STEP 3:

Double click on the rubber stamp tool, choose 50% opacity.

STEP 4:

Select ([Option/Alt]-Click) the non-bruised part of the chin and release the Mouse Button. Using this selection, even out the dark (bruised) areas of the face. Continue selection and stamping until all of the black areas are toned down. You should periodically check your work by clicking on the CMYK Channel, and visually make a judgment regarding how much work remains to be completed using the Black Channel.

STEP 5:

Once you feel that the black part of the bruised area has been removed, move to the Cyan Channel, and complete the same process.

STEP 4:

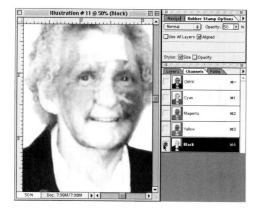

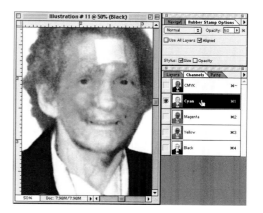

This procedure is used on every channel until the bruised area appears normal. This may involve returning to a channel previously retouched, but the important thing is to check your work periodically by clicking on the CMYK Channel.

While this method may be time consuming, it is one of the best ways to remove a bruised area without removing personal features and winding up with plastic looking skin. Other broad correction methods might remove vital characteristics from the subject such as the wrinkles and age lines in this particular case.

"... it is one of the best ways to remove a bruised area..."

Once the image is completed in the Channels process, the finishing touches to the photograph can be applied using other tools. Areas such as the bandage on the forehead in this illustration, for example, could then be removed by either using the Lasso tool or the Rubber Stamp tool.

The Channels palette is explained in greater detail in your Photoshop User's Guide and other Photoshop manuals. However, if you want more information on ways to use channels, my suggestion is that you explore this resource and discover additional uses for yourself!

4. Photoshop Filters

There are four basic filters I use consistently in digital retouching projects. These filters are: Lighting Effects Filter, Noise Filter, Gaussian Blur Filter, and Unsharp Mask Filter. It will be to your advantage to memorize the procedures for these four filters so their processes become like second nature to you. The Artistic Filters will also be covered, as they are creative tools that can be used to enhance your work when there is a need to create a painted effect.

■ Lighting Effects

Lighting Effects can be used for correcting the original light and the overall lighting contrast. This filter is used for many processes, a more common one being the equalizing of lighting in the compositing of two portraits taken under different lighting conditions. Before you begin the actual corrective work, it is important to create a Layer to complete your work on. This way you are working on a Background Copy rather than the original scanned image to produce a change in the lighting effects.

The first demonstration will show how to create shiny silver Captain's bars on a military painting. The second will demonstrate enhancement of lighting on a doggie portrait of a Poodle, and the third will show how to bring out the bride and groom's rings in a "wedding hands" portrait. First the Captain's bars. All three use the first two steps as a common opening.

Step 1:
Drag the Background Layer into the Duplicate Layer icon at the bottom of the Layer's palette.

Step 2:
Open the Lighting Effects Filter (Filter>Render>Lighting Effects).

■ Captain

The captain's bars were originally dark, almost black rather than shiny silver (see in Illustration E). It is difficult to tell they are actually silver. They were originally a part of a painted portrait that the customer wanted to have copied, converted to 11 x 14 pictures and mounted on canvas.

Step 1:
Go to the Lasso tool. Click on the small black arrow to bring up the Polygon Lasso.

"There are four basic filters I use consistently in digital retouching..."

The captain's bars were originally part of a painted portrait that the customer wanted to have copied.

E.

STEP 5A:

STEP 5B:

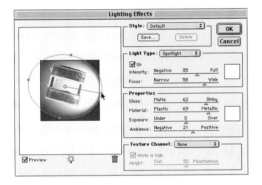

STEP 5C:

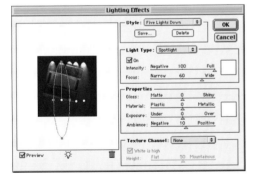

STEP 2:

Click on each corner of the captain's bars, including the indented areas.

STEP 3:

Select the inner area of the bars by depressing the Shift Key and Shift-click on the four inner corners of the cross-bars.

STEP 4:

Copy and Paste the selection into its own layer. This is the selection you will work on.

STEP 5:

Make your settings as demonstrated for the Lighting Effects window (5a). Under Properties, select Metallic, Shiny, Over-Exposed and Positive Light (5b). Change the styles of lighting by going to the Style pop-up menu (in the Lighting Effects dialogue box). For this example, Five Lights Down is chosen (5c).

    The result achieved is that the Captain's bars appear shiny silver with a 3-D effect that pops out of the picture! We will return to this image later in the chapter to demonstrate how to convert the image to appear as if it were created in a painting, with brush strokes.

STEP 2:

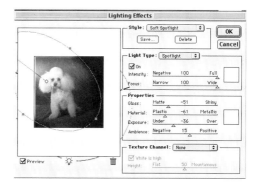

STEP 3:

■ POODLE

The poodle in this picture needs increased contrast.

STEP 1:

Select Soft Spotlight (Render>Lighting Effects>Style>Soft Spotlight) and experiment with the settings until the poodle is highlighted in a natural manner. In this case, the Properties would be Matte, Plastic, Slightly Under-Exposed and Ambience.

STEP 2:

Double click on the Lasso tool, and set the Feather Radius to 3 pixels. Using the Lasso tool, draw a loose selection around the nose and then the eyes of the dog.

STEP 3:

Once the desired areas are highlighted, press [Command/Control]+H. This hides the selection outline.

STEP 4:

Select Lighting effects (Filter>Render>Lighting Effects). This brings up the Lighting Effects dialogue box. Use Omni Light to distribute lighting evenly on the nose and the eyes.

STEP 5:

Click OK.

STEP 6:

■ HANDS

What we want to accomplish with Illustration F is to highlight the hands without disturbing the rest of the background. In order to accomplish this, we will use the Magnetic Lasso tool.

STEP 1:
Select the Magnetic Lasso from the tool box. To do this, click the Lasso tool to bring up the extended Lasso menu. The Magnetic Lasso tool has a small magnet on it.

STEP 2:
Drag the Lasso around both the bride's and groom's hands, continuing back to where you started. When the cursor changes to signify that the loop is closed, release the mouse button.

STEP 3:
To fine tune the selected area, zoom in and switch to Quick Mask, located in the bottom right side of the tool box.

Our job is to highlight the hands without losing detail in the background.

F.

STEP 3: AFTER SWITCHING TO QUICK MASK

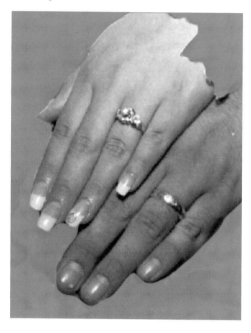

STEP 4:

Use the Eraser and the Paint Brush to ensure a crisp, clean selection of just the hands. Once this is accomplished, switch back to standard mode (the button on the toolbar is pictured below).

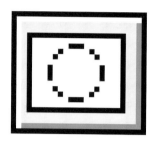

STEP 5:

Select the Crossing Down Lighting Effect (Filter>Render> Lighting Effects>Style>Crossing Down).

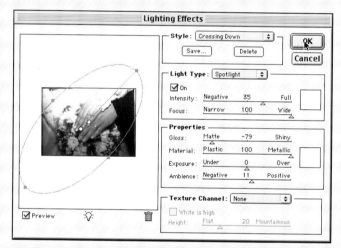

The two small white circles on the screen represent individual lights. Normally the default setting is two Spotlights. In this example, the light types will be set to Spotlight and Omni. The white circle identifies where the intensity of light is focused. Click-dragging on the white circle adjusts the light. The larger black circle brightens or dims the light. The handles can be used to narrow or widen the circle by clicking and dragging.

STEP 6:

Set one light on Spotlight, using it to brighten the ring and to enhance the overall lighting. Focus it just below the bride's ring to avoid unnecessary glare. Play with this to determine what looks best.

STEP 7:

Adjust the Intensity setting until you achieve an even lighting effect. Refer to the screen shot for settings of the various slider adjustments.

"Adjust the Intensity setting until you achieve an even lighting effect."

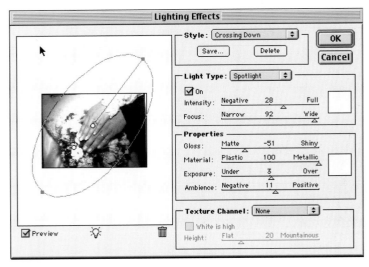

STEP 8:

Click on the little white circle that represents the second light. Change it to the Spotlight setting.

STEP 9:

Click on the Anchor at the top of the black circle where the Tether connects the light with the outer circle, and drag the Tether around to the bottom Anchor. This will change the direction of the light. Adjust this lighting so the light evenly covers the hand while bringing out the beauty of the bride's ring, then click OK. Remove the selection [Command/Control]+D.

▪ USING THE NOISE FILTER

The Noise Filter is a useful tool to replace the grainy features characteristic of human skin. In Illustration G you will notice that the cheek of this beautiful bride is very smooth.

STEP 1:

Zoom into the bride's cheek area.

STEP 2:

Double-click the Rubber Stamp tool. Choose 20% Opacity.

STEP 3:

Select Show Brushes from the Windows menu and choose a Soft brush.

USING NOISE CAN HELP RESTORE CHARACTERISTICS TO SKIN.

G.

STEP 4:

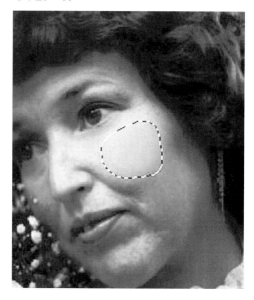

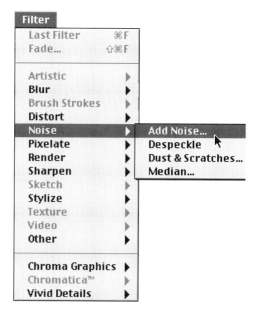

EXPERIMENT WITH SETTINGS:

Check out the higher numbers while you are here just to experiment and learn the difference!

STEP 4:

Outline a section of the area to correct with the Lasso tool, designate 10 pixels in the Feather Option Box. This will provide you with a soft edge.

STEP 5:

Choose Add Noise. And the Add Noise dialogue box will appear.

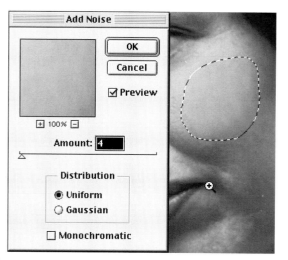

STEP 6:

Choose a low number in Amount selection. Select the Uniform radial button in the Distribution box.

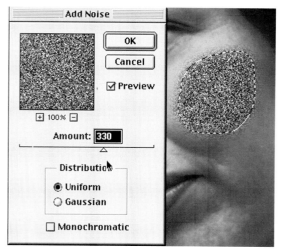

STEP 7:

Deselect.

STEP 8:

Add noise to other areas of the image to finish the project.

"The term Gaussian comes from a photographic technique."

The optimum time to apply the Noise Filter is after all other retouching on the image has been completed. [Command/ Control]+F automatically selects the last Filter used, so the keystroke can be used to apply the Noise filter and identical settings to other areas.

■ WHEN TO USE GAUSSIAN BLUR

The term Gaussian comes from a photographic technique. The technique involves the placing of a piece of regular gauze in front of the lens or stretch it over wire (such as a coat hanger) and pass it under the lens during the darkroom negative exposure to soften the picture through light diffusion. Photoshop's Gaussian Blur Filter creates the same effect in digital retouching.

Applying the Gaussian Blur Filter can result in a blurry, mannequin-like effect on the skin texture. So, when is it appropriate to use Gaussian Blur? The answer to this question can be explored in returning to the hands of the bride and groom.

STEP 1:

Double-Click on the Marquee tool to open the Options Box.

STEP 2:

Set the Feather option at 20, and make sure Anti-alias is checked.

STEP 3:

Select the elliptical Marquee tool, by clicking and holding the Mouse Button down on the Marquee tool icon.

STEP 4:

Click and Drag the Elliptical Marquee tool until it forms a circle around the hands and flowers.

STEP 5:

Invert the selection in order to blur the portion of the image outside the circle rather than the hands (push [Command/Control]+[Shift]+I keys all at the same time).

STEP 6:

Hide the Marching Ants (push [Command/Control]+H or choose View>Hide Edges).

STEP 7:

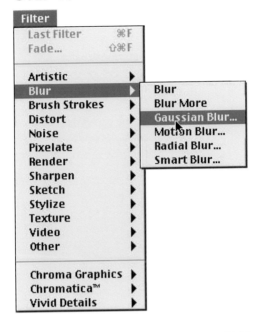

STEP 7:

Blur the image (Filter>Blur>Gaussian Blur). In the Gaussian Blur dialogue box be sure to check the Preview selection. In the Radius selection play with the Pixels selection to see what looks best.

Once you have achieved the desired effect and the OK button is pushed, you have your final image. Please note that the image in this illustration is a 300 dpi image, thus would require a higher pixel selection than a smaller size image.

This tool is particularly useful for creating a different background without importing any new type of image. Be creative and use the Gaussian Blur tool any way you find it useful!

■ UNSHARP MASK – SHARPENING YOUR IMAGE

Let's return to the picture of the German Shepherd. Since the original picture was somewhat blurred, you can apply the Unsharp filter.

STEP 1:

Open the Unsharp Mask dialogue box (Filter Menu> Sharpen>Unsharp Mask).

STEP 2:

Use the sliders to adjust the sharpness of the image. Be careful not to over sharpen the picture. Then click OK.

DON'T OVERSHARPEN:

Use Unsharp Mask with caution. This tool can be overused easily.

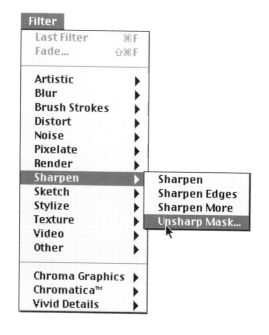

In this particular image I sharpened the complete photograph since the whole picture was somewhat blurred. Note the difference in the two images of the dog.

■ USING FILTERS

■ DRY BRUSH

Return to the Captain's Bars (Illustration E). Even though they appeared very shiny and nice when we left off, they are part of a painting, and therefore need to have the appearance of brush strokes in order to blend in to the total perspective.

STEP 1:
Recall the selection of the bars using the saved selection, or retrace it using the Lasso tool.

STEP 2:
Open the Dry Brush filter (Filter Menu>Artistic>Dry Brush). The Dry Brush pallet appears.

STEP 3:
Play with the sliders, experimenting with the different settings until the image appears as desired. Once the you achieve the desired effect, click on the OK button.

STEP 4:
To match the grain on the original canvas, open the Film Grain filter (Filter Menu>Artistic>Film Grain). Use the sliders to blend the bars perfectly with the rest of the painting.

STEP 5:
Once the blending is complete, flatten the image ([Command/Control]+E).

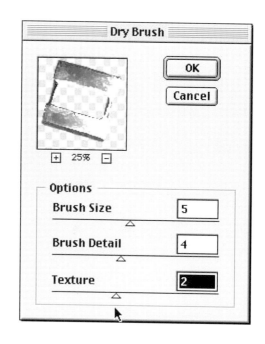

STEP 4:

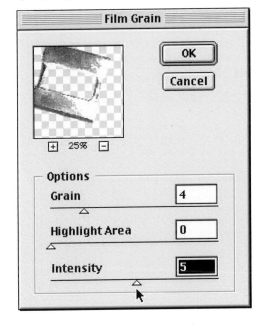

STEP 2:

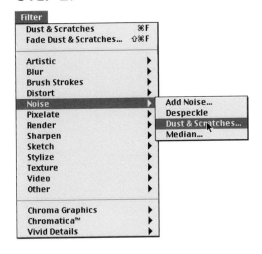

■ USING THE DUST AND SCRATCHES FILTER

Old photographs are often received with multiple scratches, stains, and fingerprints. A scan may result in an image covered with dust spots. To remove these problems quickly, we will look at the Dust and Scratches filter and how to apply it to different shots. Do not apply this filter to the whole photograph at once - it could result in an image that has a "painted" appearance because it blurs the pixels. Used on small areas, it can be a very useful tool!

STEP 1:
Open your image in Photoshop.

STEP 2:
Open the Dust and Scratches Filter (Filter>Noise>Dust and Scratches).

STEP 3:

Select a small area that contains dust and scratches using the Lasso tool, and open the Dust and Scratches Filter. You can work on each area individually, or you can select a number of areas to be corrected by holding down the Shift Key while using the Lasso tool. Avoid selecting areas that contain a lot of specific detail (e.g. eyes, some hair, etc.)

5. CREATIVE PHOTO ENHANCEMENT

■ COLOR RANGE SELECTION TOOL

The Color Range Selection tool allows you to select portions of an image based on color. The primary difference between this tool and the Replace Color selection is that the Color Range Selection tool has the option of deselecting areas that you do not want to change.

"The Color Range Selection tool allows you to select portions of an image based on color."

H.

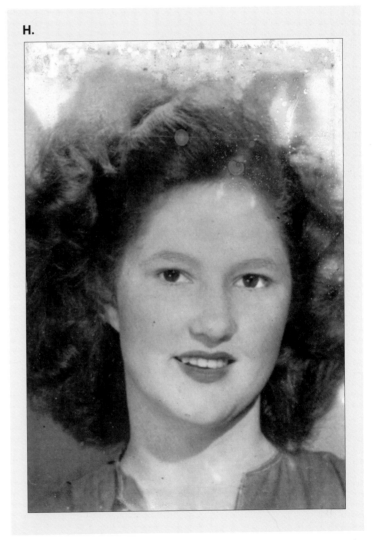

Illustration H is an old colored photo that has rust stains in various parts of the hair.

STEP 1:

Open Color Range (Selection Menu>Color Range). The Color Range dialogue box appears on the screen.

STEP 1:

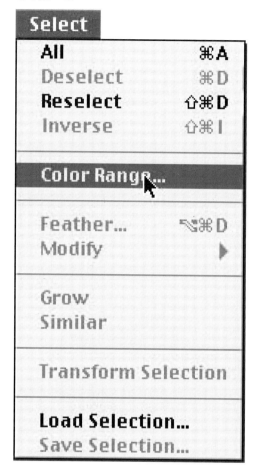

STEP 2:

Move the eye-dropper cursor over to the image on top of the area you want to change.

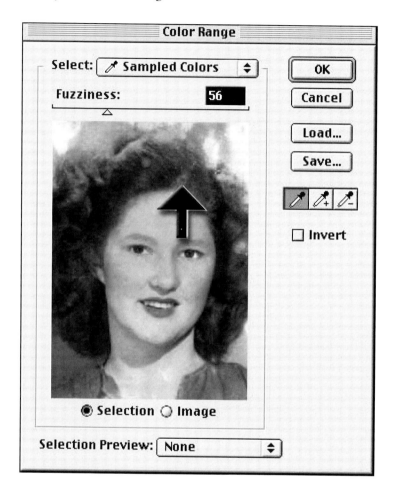

STEP 3:

Click the mouse button with the eye dropper cursor over the red spot on the image. Then click OK. All of the red areas are now selected and outlined.

STEP 4:

Press [Command/Control]+H to hide the outline.

STEP 5:

Press [Command/Control]+B to open Color Balance (or Image>Adjust>Color Balance).

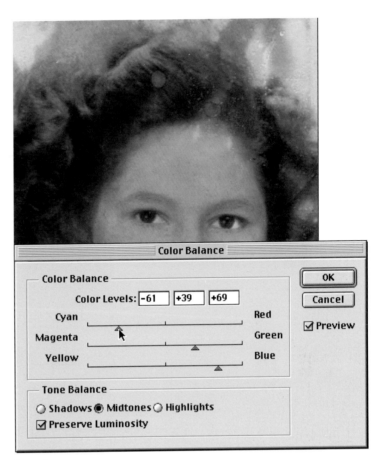

STEP 7:

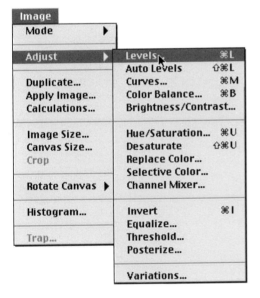

STEP 8:

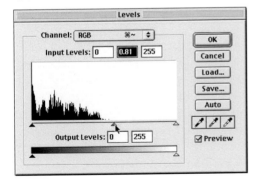

STEP 6:
Adjust the sliders to refine the color. Continue to correct using all three of the radial options (Shadows, Highlights, and Midtones) until the red is gone.

STEP 7:
Open Levels ([Command/Control]+L or Image>Adjust> Levels).

STEP 8:
Adjust by moving the middle slider under Input Levels to the right until the middle reading is 0.81, and the spot blends in.

STEP 9:
Press [Command/Control]+D to Deselect.

If you need to fine-tune the color (in this case a red ring is still visible around the outer perimeter of the previously red stained areas), return to the Color Range dialogue menu. Click on the eyedropper, and click on each ring. This will select a number of corresponding areas with similar color once again. Using the Lasso tool, select and delete the areas you don't want to change. Repeat the process in the steps above. This is a good time to use Replace Color and finalize the correction. We will be revisiting the use of this tool in Illuminating Shadows.

"This is a good time to use Replace Color and finalize the correction."

■ CREATING THE PERFECT BACKGROUND

You can import images from CDs to use as backgrounds, but there are also many ways to change the existing background to something totally different using various filters and your own creativity.

In Illustration I, a customer wanted to display a portrait of a recently deceased woman. There were no recent pictures of just her, so she needed to be isolated from another image to get what the customer wanted. The replacement for the background is right in the image; the existing background seen through the window can be used.

I will be using a process that is somewhat involved and can be done more simply by another method. However, this method demonstrates the use of various tools and will help your understanding of such processes.

"... this method demonstrates the use of various tools..."

I.

STEP 1:
Open the Layer's palette.

STEP 2:
Select the Lasso tool, double-click on it, and set the Feather Radius to 0.

STEP 3:
Loosely select the primary subject.

STEP 4:
Copy and Paste to place the selection in its own layer.

STEP 5:

Select the Move tool (Press "V" Key).

STEP 6:

Move the image of the primary subject over to the right on top of the secondary subject. The lady should be sitting next to herself in the image.

STEP 9A:

STEP 9B:

STEP 7:

Turn the eye icon for Layer 1 in the Layers palette off by clicking on it.

STEP 8:

Double-click on the Lasso tool, and set the Feather Radius to 10 pixels.

STEP 9C:

STEP 9:

Hold down the [Command/Control]+ [Option/Alt] keys while using the Lasso tool. Select parts of the background and begin covering the second woman and window (9a and 9b). Extend the background until both are completely covered. Remember to maintain the integrity of the lines in the background as it is expanded.

Another effective way to do this is to use the Marquee tool, with a Feather Radius of 20 pixels (9c).

STEP 10:

Erase the parts of the Layer around the primary subject that still show the brick wall by clicking on Layer 1 to activate it, and using a small, hard-edged brush with the Eraser tool. Make sure the Eraser Options dialogue box is set to 100%.

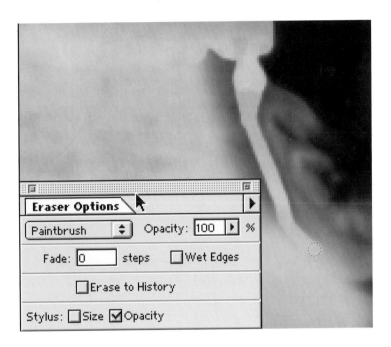

If you make a mistake while erasing, borrow parts from the background to produce the final result you desire.

STEP 11:

Crop the image by using the Crop tool. Drag the Anchor until the subject's nose is somewhat the central focus of the picture, then press Enter/Return.

STEP 11:

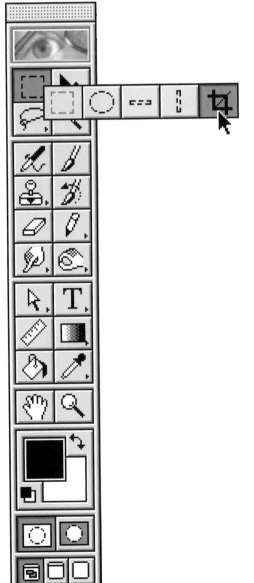

STEP 12:

Flatten the image, and this job is complete.

"... you might want to add a border..."

■ ADDING A BORDER

To enhance an existing background, you might want to add a border to it. This can be done in a couple of ways. There are many programs and plug-ins that will create borders. But the creative Photoshop user can add his/her own. For this example, we will go back to the portrait of Buffie the poodle.

STEP 1:

Draw a loose selection around the outer edge of the picture by using the Lasso tool, making sure the selection is non-symmetrical.

STEP 2:
Once the border area is selected, save the selection.

STEP 5:

STEP 6:

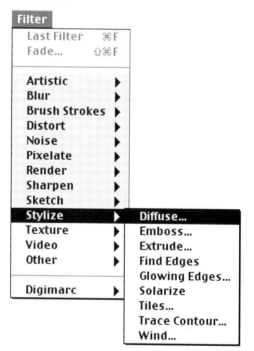

STEP 3:

Go to Show Channels (Window Menu> Channels>Show Channels).

STEP 4:

Deselect.

STEP 5:

Click on the Alpha Channel to select it as your active channel. Your image will disappear (temporarily) and all you see is a black border.

STEP 6:

Open the Diffuse filter (Filters>Stylize>Diffuse). This brings up a Diffuse dialogue box. Make sure you are in the Normal Mode. Click OK if the previews are acceptable.

STEP 7:

Zoom in to check on your work.

STEP 8:

Intensify the effect by pressing [Command/Control]+F, repeating until the border appears to have a burned look around the edge.

STEP 9:

Open the Gaussian Blur filter (Filter>Blur> Gaussian Blur). When the Gaussian Blur dialogue box appears, set the Radius to 1.0 pixel. When you apply the blur, it softens and blends the edges of the area into the background.

STEP 10:

Go to the Channels palette, and click/drag the Alpha 1 channel into the Load Channel (dotted circle at bottom left of Channels palette as a Selection Icon at the bottom of the palette. This loads your Alpha Channel as a selection. Click on the RGB Channel to bring the image of the poodle back into focus with a selection around the edge of the image.

STEP 11:

Invert the selection (Select Menu>Inverse) and press the Delete Key.

"This loads your Alpha Channel as a selection."

STEP 12:

Drag the channel to the bottom of the Channels palette to select just the dog image.

STEP 13:

Select the rectangular Marquee tool and set the radius to 20.

STEP 15:

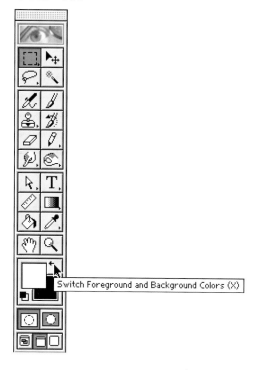

STEP 17:

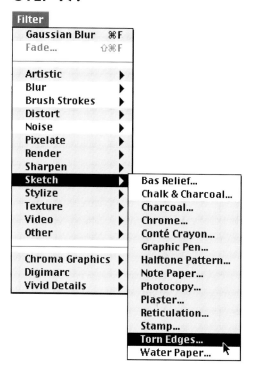

STEP 14:

Hold down [Option/Alt] and drag the cursor from the top left corner to the bottom of the image within the background of the dog until you have a square selection that remains within the blue background.

STEP 15:

Open the Color Picker tool and switch the the Foreground and Background colors by clicking on the arrow. This will switch the swatches so that the white square is on the top and the black square is on the bottom.

STEP 16:

Click Delete. A black border will appear.

STEP 17:

Go to (Filter>Sketch>Torn Edges) to summon the Torn Edges dialogue.

STEP 18:

Set Image Balance to 17, Smoothness to 3, and Contrast to 2. You may want to experiment with the settings a little.

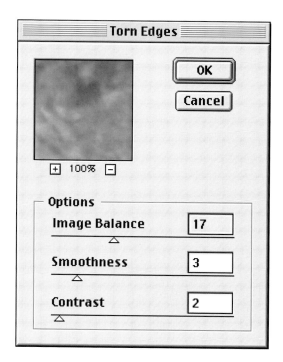

STEP 19:

Drag the Alpha channel to the Trash located at the bottom of the Channels Palette.

PREPPING IMAGES FOR PRINT

Before you send an image to a lab or service bureau, be sure that all extra layers and channels are deleted and the image is flattened.

D.

■ CREATING CLOUDS

For an example of creating a new background using Clouds, return to Illustration D.

STEP 1:
Double-click on the Magic Wand tool, and set the Tolerance to 85 in the Options dialogue. Make sure the Anti-aliased box is checked.

STEP 2:
Place the cursor in the white area and click once. This will select the background area, except for the frame.

STEP 3:
Open the Lasso tool. Make sure the Feather Radius is set to 0.

STEP 7:

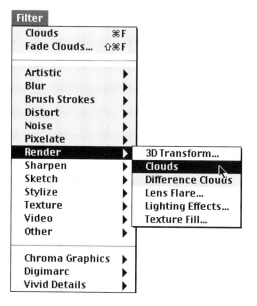

STEP 4:

Hold down the Shift key while selecting the right part of the lady's shoulder, and move up to the top and over to the edge of the frame. The shoulder selection joins the selection of the edge of the frame.

STEP 5:

Click on the Mask tool. This will allow you to fine-tune your selection.

STEP 6:

Open the Color Picker from the swatches on the tool bar, and choose colors for the foreground and background. Any combination of colors can be used. A more obvious effect is created by using colors with greater contrast.

STEP 7:

Open the Clouds filter (Filter Menu>Render> Clouds). This will create a subtle cloud background for this image.

STEP 8:

Use the Smudge tool with a Small Brush Size to soften the edges, especially around the hair.

■ CREATING SHADOWS

Occasionally shadows enhance photographic effects. In the example we will be considering, a shadowing effect under the chin enhances the natural beauty of the subject.

STEP 4:

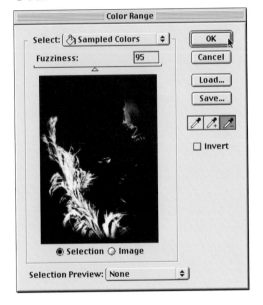

COLOR RANGE SELECTIONS

When the red feathers are selected, be aware that this program will also select any other areas with similar colors!

STEP 1:

Select Color Range (Menu>Color Range). This brings up the Color Range dialogue box.

STEP 2:

Be sure the Selection radial button has been chosen, then click on the red feathers to select them. Move the slider until the feathers all appear white (the image will appear in a black & white format).

STEP 3:

Set the Selection Preview to Black Masque to see your selection more clearly. When you are satisfied with the selection, change the Selection Preview back to None, and click OK.

STEP 4:

Now move to the Lasso tool, and hold down the [Option/Alt] key while deselecting what you don't want selected (i.e., the cheeks and lipstick).

STEP 5:

Copy and Paste the image of the feathers into its own Layer.

"Copy and Paste the image of the feathers into its own Layer."

STEP 6:

Select the Lasso tool and draw a circle around the shadowed part of the woman's cheek.

STEP 7:

Copy and Paste the cheek into its own Layer.

STEP 8:

Press [Command/Control]+T to open the Transform tool.

STEP 9:

Stretch the shadowed area over the back part of the cheek to cover the highlights.

STEP 10:

Drag the existing layer to the Copy icon at the bottom of the Layers Palette. This creates two identical layers that can be used together once they are joined to provide a larger coverage area. Press [Command/Control]+E keys to join the two layers together. This allows you to use these sections of skin jointly to cover a larger area.

STEP 11:
Turn off the eye next to the Background Layer, by clicking on it. Smooth out this layer so the skin texture is even by using the Rubber Stamp tool.

STEP 12:
Select the shadow area right under the chin with the Lasso tool to create another layer for shadow coverage. Copy and Paste this selection into its own layer ([Command/Control] +C, [Command/ Control]+V).

STEP 13:
Move the shadow into place on the left side of the lower neck. Open Free Transform (Edit>Free Transform) to stretch the shadow you just created in this new layer.

STEP 14:
Select the Lasso tool. Using the Lasso tool, select the long skinny top part of part of the layer you are working on and Copy and Paste to create a new chin line.

STEP 15:
Stretch the newest layer up to meet the other shadow using the Transform tool ([Command/Control]+T).

STEP 16:
Switch to the Background Layer, then select part of the feathers and shoulder using the Lasso tool with a Radius of 10.

STEP 17:
Hold down the [Command/Control] keys and move the selection up to cover the part of the shoulder. You might want to use a similar technique to fill in areas of the hair.

While this image looks good as it is, the shadows under the eyes remain a distraction and can be enhanced by illumination.

■ ILLUMINATING SHADOWS

The areas under the eyes and chin in Illustration J need to be lightened to improve the image.

STEP 1:
Magnify the picture by using the Zoom tool.

WHICH METHOD TO USE:

The important thing to remember in using Photoshop is that there are multiple ways to accomplish the same task. It is not really important which method you use, as long as you accomplish the desired outcome.

Lightening the shadows in this image will soften the subject's features.

J.

STEP 2:

Open the Rubber Stamp tool and set the Opacity to 20.

STEP 3:

Select a brush approximately the size (vertical width) of the the dark areas under the eyes.

STEP 4:

[Option/Alt]+Click in the highlighted area on the cheek on the left side of the image. Use this as the skin to clone from.

STEP 5:

Clone to the area under the left eye.

STEP 6:

Move to the right side and complete the same process.

"Click in the highlighted area on the cheek..."

Buffie the poodle could benefit from a similar technique. The last image of Buffie (page 33) shows her with a shadow underneath that can be toned down or removed.

STEP 1:
Open Color Range (Select>Color Range).

STEP 2:
Move the Eye Dropper cursor to the shadow area and click on the shadow, then click OK.

STEP 3:
Use the Lasso tool to deselect areas you do not want. Press the [Option/Alt] key, hold down the mouse button and outline the unwanted selections.

STEP 4:
Press [Command/Control]+L to bring up Levels (Image File>Menu>Adjust>Levels). The Level's dialogue box appears.

STEP 5:
Move the middle slider until the shadow is toned down and appears acceptable. Click the OK Button.

STEP 3:

K.

LAYERS PALETTE:

It is probably best to consistently work with the Layer's palette open.

The same processes used in Dodging and Burning Techniques Using Channels will be used to illuminate the shadows in Illustration K. The primary difference between these examples is that in this one we are dealing with a major shadowed area. We will lighten the shadows on the man's face and shirt by a process of Illumination.

STEP 1:
Press [Option/Alt] and click on the Create New Layer icon in the Layers palette. A New Layer dialogue box will appear.

STEP 2:
In the Mode pop-up menu, select Soft Light. Select the Fill with Soft-Light-neutral color (50% gray) check box, and click OK. This brings up a neutral gray layer.

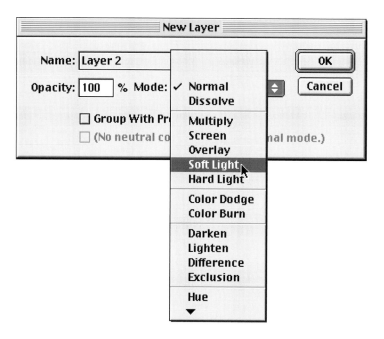

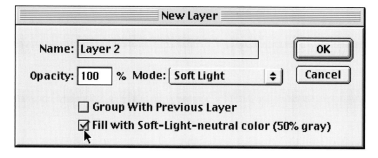

STEP 3:
Show Swatches (Window Menu>Show Swatches).

STEP 4:

Double-click on the Airbrush tool. Set the Pressure to 20 in the Options dialogue.

STEP 5:

Magnify the picture with the Zoom tool.

STEP 6:

[Option/Alt]+Click with the cursor on the lightest part of the subject's right fist.

STEP 7:

Paint on the unwanted shadow area using the Airbrush until the shadow is significantly reduced.

STEP 8:

Use the Swatches palette to select the color to paint the shirt, and paint that in too.

STEP 9:

Merge the layers [Command/Control]+E.

STEP 10:

Open the Rubber Stamp tool. Rubber Stamp tool will be used to tone down the line left from the shadow. Use the rubber stamp tool to draw from the highlighted area into the shadow area, toning the shadow area down.

STEP 11:

Add a little Noise to the area where the shadow was, using the Lasso tool to select the area. You can easily see the difference between the beginning and the final results below.

SWATCHES USE:

I do not like to use the Color Swatches for skin tone because it is difficult to produce a natural appearing skin tone.

"This operation brings together a number of processes we have already covered."

■ DROP SHADOWS

This operation brings together a number of processes we have already covered. The original job was to take the distractions out of the background of the image with the fine Arabian show horse in illustration L. Then the breeder decided the display needed a different background. The ultimate process will not only involve moving the horse into a different background, but creating a drop shadow to complete the illusion. The most difficult and tedious task involved in this project is selecting the tail from the background.

L.

STEP 1:
Roughly select the animal using the Lasso tool.

STEP 2:
Click on the Quick Mask tool. This covers the horse with a red mask.

STEP 3:
Magnify the image to 300% and toggle back and forth between the Eraser tool and the Paint tool to create a tight mask for the horse.

STEP 4:
Convert the mask into a selection by switching out of Quick Mask.

STEP 5:
Open the new background for this mare.

MASKING PLUG-INS

There are plug-ins that are designed for just the purpose of masking, but they do not complete the task in the quality manner required by photo retouching.

"Transform the horse to a smaller size..."

STEP 18:

STEP 6:

Activate the window for the horse by clicking on it.

STEP 7:

Select the Move tool.

STEP 8:

Transform the horse to a smaller size to fit in the final picture. Press [Command/Control]+T to call up the Transform function.

STEP 9:

Position the horse in the desired location in the background picture.

STEP 10:

Copy the horse layer by dragging it into the Duplicate icon at the bottom of the Layer's palette. This creates a duplicate copy of this image in its own layer.

STEP 11:

Drag the copy under the original.

STEP 12:

Click on the Eye Icon next to Layer 1 to turn off that layer.

STEP 13:

Open the Levels dialogue box.

STEP 14:

Move all Slider settings to the far right to fill the image on the duplicate layer with black.

STEP 15:

Flip the image 180° (Edit Menu> Transform>Vertical). This results in the black image being turned upside down in the background picture.

STEP 16:

Click the Eye Icon on Layer 1 to bring the horse back into the picture.

STEP 17:

Press [Command/Control]+T, then hold down the [Command/Control] key while moving the anchors into place to distort the shadow.

STEP 18:

Drag the image to the appropriate place so hooves match to hooves.

STEP 20:

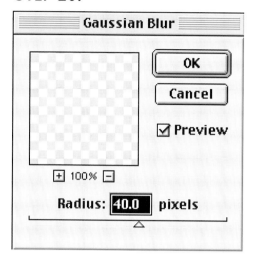

STEP 19:

Continue to manipulate the shadow until it appears appropriate for the lighting. When you have accomplished this, press Enter to apply the Transformation.

STEP 20:

Open Gaussian Blur. Play with the Radius setting until the horse shadow density matches the density of the existing shadows. Click OK.

STEP 21:

The Rubber Stamp tool should be used to reduce some of the highlights and to remove the bridle.

6. BLACK & WHITE IMAGES

Most of the truly old pictures that come to the retouching and restoration artist are either black & white or brown tone. Regardless of how old they are, they are likely to be in poor shape and in need of significant work. Regardless of the condition, the customer is bringing this picture to a professional to get it repaired. When working with black & white pictures it is important to keep in mind that these images are composed of levels of grayscale that vary from pure black to pure white. This job is difficult and time-consuming, but typical of many restoration jobs.

"This job is difficult and time-consuming, but typical of many restoration jobs."

STEP 4:

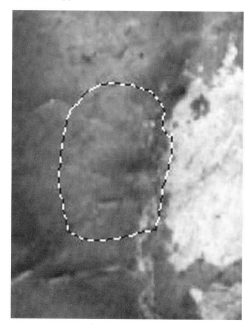

■ HOW TO REPLACE MISSING PIECES

STEP 1:
Scan the image into Photoshop.

STEP 2:
Save a copy of the original scan.

STEP 3:
Magnify the mouth area.

STEP 4:
Use the Lasso tool to select an area around the intact part of the mouth.

STEP 5:
Copy and Paste the selected area.

STEP 6:
Flip Horizontal (Edit Menu>Transform>Flip Horizontal).

STEP 7:
Press [Command/Control]+T (Transform).

STEP 8:
Drag it to the right side of the face to the approximate location where the lip would fit.

STEP 9:

Holding the cursor outside of the Bounding Box results in a double-headed arrow which rotates the selection. Rotate the Bounding Box until the top and bottom of the box align with the line of her eyes. Then press the [Enter/Return] Key.

STEP 10:

Be sure that Layer 1 is highlighted. Use the Opacity Slider to match the skin tone and the newly created mouth area.

STEP 11:

Open the Rubber Stamp tool. Begin the process of sampling from the lips on the left side of the image to recreate the missing part of the mouth. This process can be enhanced by using the Lasso tool to Select, Copy and Paste from the right side of the image, or the upper lip to the lower lip.

STEP 12:

Smooth out some of the skin tone areas using the Rubber Stamp tool with a low Opacity (30 or lower).

"Smooth out some of the skin tone areas using the Rubber Stamp..."

STEP 13:

Select a portion of the nose and Copy and Paste.

STEP 14:

Flip Horizontal (Edit Menu>Transform>Flip Horizontal) and move it into the area you want to end up. The same process is also used to fill in the cheek area.

"This small setting feathers the selection area..."

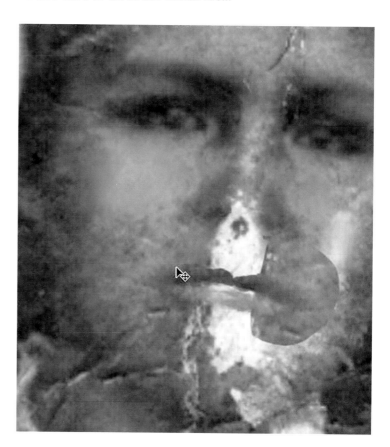

STEP 16:

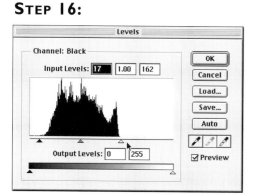

STEP 15:

Open Levels.

STEP 16:

Drag the light arrow (slider) over to the edge of the black density area, and the black arrow (slider) inward to the edge of the black area to increase density, and press OK.

STEP 17:

Open the Lasso tool, and set the Feather Radius to 5 pixels. This small setting feathers the selection area rather than creating a hard line. Make sure you are working on Layer 1.

"Continue this drag and drop process until the area is filled."

STEP 18:

Hold down [Command/Control] and the [Option/Alt] keys to drag small selections of skin close to the area being replaced. Continue this drag and drop process until the area is filled. In this particular area, it is important to keep in perspective that the area under the nose contains peaks and a valley. The valley area would be more shadowed than the peaked area. You can borrow shadow area from any dark area (i.e., on the nose bridge) to create the shadow effect. Do not be concerned about the blending at this point. We will blend later with the Rubber Stamp tool.

STEP 4:

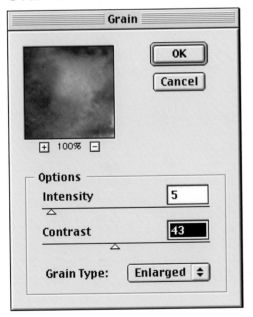

STEP 19:

Open the Grain dialogue box (Filter>Texture>Grain). Set the Intensity to 5, the Contrast to 43, and the Grain Type to Enlarged.

STEP 20:

Select the highlighted area of the cheek on the left side of the the image from the background using the Lasso.

STEP 21:

Copy and Paste.

STEP 22:

Drag the selected area down to the chin holding down [Command/Control].

STEP 23:

Set the Opacity for this Layer to 67% or 68% to blend with the skin tone, creating shadow and highlight on the chin.

STEP 24:

Continue to blend the skin area on the Background Layer using the Rubber Stamp.

DUPLICATING SELECTIONS:

If you continue to hold down the Command/Control and the Option/Alt Keys you can drag and drop the same selection in a number of areas.

STEP 25:

Using the Lasso tool, select an area on the hair to the right of the scratch, hold down the [Command/Control]+[Option/Alt] keys, drag and drop the selected area over the scratch.

STEP 26:

Once the face is basically retouched, Flatten the Layers.

STEP 27:

Create a new layer to work on by holding down the [Option/Alt] key while clicking on the Duplicate Layers icon.

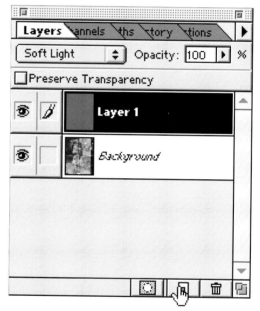

STEP 28:

Press [Command/Control]+E to merge this layer into the Background Layer.

STEP 29:

Before you finish with the face, return to the Filter Menu ([Command/Control]+F) and run the Grain Filter over the whole face.

STEP 30:

Use Drag and Drop to repair the entire photograph, filling the cracks as you go.

It is important to play with the varied textures as you work on various areas of this picture. For example, once you finish the dress, try using the grain texture on it to unsmooth it, giving it a more real appearance. This is also true of the sweater.

DUPLICATE THE BACKGROUND:

It is helpful to create a duplicate of the Background Layer to work on. If you find you do not like what is happening, you can easily start over by throwing the duplicate layer away and beginning over with another Background Layer.

"... turn this black & white picture into a duotone.

■ CREATING DUOTONES

We will use the illustration from the previous example to demonstrate how to turn this b&w picture into a duotone.

STEP 1:
Open the image.

STEP 2:
Switch the mode to duotone (Menu>Mode>Duotone). A Duotone Options dialogue box appears.

STEP 3:
Select the Duotone option in the pop-up menu. This allows you to apply two inks to the image.

STEP 4:
Click on the Ink 1 color swatch square, and select a Black color. Then click on the Ink 2 color swatch square, and select PANTONE 1365 CVC as the second color choice. The Overprint Colors can be readily seen along the bottom of the dialogue box. Click OK. This will automatically transform the picture to the duotone picture color.

■ COLORING BLACK-AND-WHITE PHOTOGRAPHS

This technique combines existing color and hand tinting. The color image of the bride and groom will be placed into the b&w image of the wedding cake.

"This technique combines existing color and hand tinting."

STEP 1:
Open both images on the screen.

STEP 2:
Move each image to its own separate layers.

STEP 3:
Convert the b&w image to color (Image>Mode> RGB).

STEP 4:
Drag the image of the bride and groom into the area above the top of the cake.

STEP 5:
Press [Command/Control]+T. Click and Drag the anchor on the bottom right hand corner to enlarge the size of the image of the bride and groom until it appears proportionate to the cake top. Move the image by dragging if necessary.

STEP 6:
When the image is in the appropriate place, press Enter to accept the Transformation.

STEP 7:
Open the Airbrush Options dialogue box by double clicking on the tool.

STEP 8:

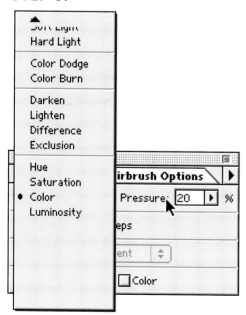

STEP 8:
Select a turquoise color in the color picker.

STEP 9:

Set Opacity to 20%.

STEP 10:

Select a small, soft brush about the width of the ribbon.

STEP 11:

Begin painting in the ribbons with the airbrush. Color the ribbons that are obviously behind the veil lightly. Use a soft-edged brush.

"Begin painting in the ribbons with the airbrush."

The same principle illustrated in this example would be used to color any part of a photograph.

▪ VARIATIONS

Variations is a pull-down menu item that is a very helpful process for comparing colors.

STEP 1:

Open Variations (Image Menu>Adjust>Variations).

STEP 1:

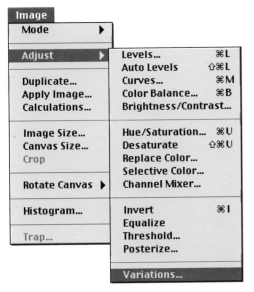

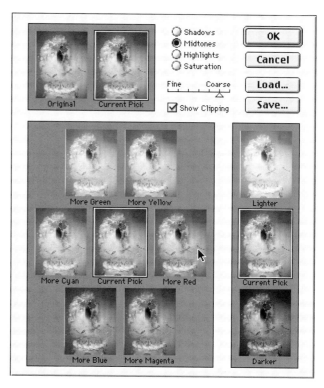

M.

N.

STEP 2:

Once the function is open, play with the various combinations of setting.

STEP 3:

Choose more Red and more Yellow to produce a Sepia Tone image (making it almost golden in color) and select OK.

■ IMPORTING SKIN TONE

Two basic ways to get realistic skin tones onto black-and-white images are to use skin tones from the same person in another image, or draw upon images available of other people. This correction draws skin tones from a bridal image M taken about 13 years earlier than Illustration N.

STEP 1:

Open both images.

STEP 2:

Double-click the Airbrush tool. Select 20% Opacity in the options when the pallet opens.

STEP 3:

Click on the color image to select it.

Sepia toning often works well with old photos.

O.

STEP 2:

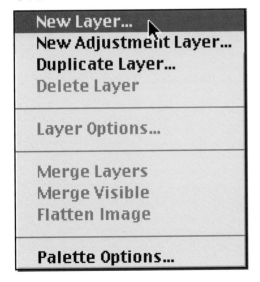

STEP 4:
Choose a large, soft brush.

STEP 5:
[Option/Alt] Click on a light area of skin under the eye on the color image.

STEP 6:
Paint the skin areas on the subject. Zoom in as necessary. To intensify the color (e.g. in the shadow areas), paint over the same area more than once. For areas such as the lips, another color can be selected. Do not go to darker colors as you might do in a hand oil or dye colorization process.

When you do not have a color image of the subject, use a color image from a collection of CD Photos or even from the Internet. The important thing is to select a skin tone that is similar to the skin tone of the subject. When completing the image, make sure all skin areas are covered in the original b&w image.

■ TRUE SEPIA TONE EFFECTS

The purpose in this process is to sharpen the features of the subjects in the image by creating a mask of the highlighted areas. For this exercise we will use the image in Illustration O.

STEP 1:
Convert the grayscale image to color (Image>Mode>RGB Color).

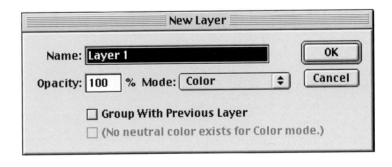

STEP 2:
Create a new layer (Layers palette pull-down Menu: New Layer>Color).

STEP 3:
Click on the Color Picker in the tool box. Set the following selections in the Select Foreground Color selections: H - 25, S - 98, and B - 36. This will be a browntone color. You can

experiment with other settings to see the impact of these color selections on your final image.

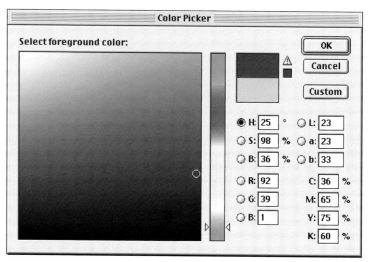

"You will now have an image with a sepia-tone effect."

Step 4:

Select an area you desire to color.

Step 5:

Press [Option/Alt]+Delete to fill the selected Layer with the color you have chosen. You will now have an image with a sepia-tone effect.

Step 6:

Go to Calculations (Image>Calculations). This brings up a Calculations dialogue box.

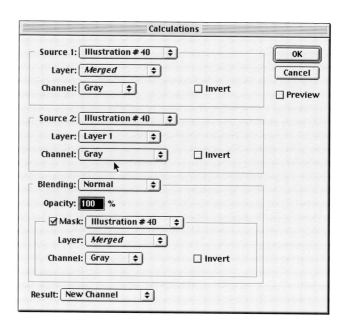

STEP 7:

Under Source 1, the setting should read Merged in Layer, and Gray in Channel. Source 2 should also read Gray in the Channel setting. Blending is set at Normal, Opacity at 100%.

STEP 8:

Check the mask, and making sure the number or title matches Source 1 and 2. Layer should be Merged, and Channel should be Gray. The Result will be New Channel.

STEP 9:

Choose Load Selection (Select>Load Selection) to bring up the Load Selection dialogue. Click OK.

STEP 10:

[Command/Control]+L brings up the Levels palette.

"This will provide a more subtle sepia tone..."

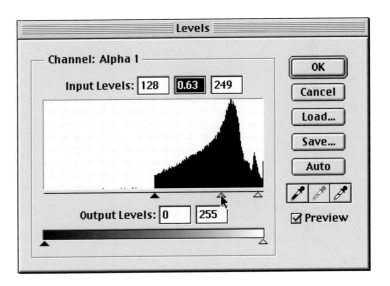

STEP 11:

Push Input Levels sliders to the right, and far right slider to the left to highlight the colors, and click OK.

STEP 12:

At the top of the Channels palette, click on RGB Channel.

STEP 13:

Desaturate the image area (Image>Adjust> Desaturate).

STEP 14:

Merge these Layers by pressing [Command/ Control]+E, and Save your work. This will provide a more subtle sepia tone print as a final result.

7. ADVANCED RETOUCHING METHODS

While you should be relatively familiar with basic operations that have been covered in previous sections, the following advanced techniques do not assume the user has advanced skills.

■ REMOVING BACKGROUND IMAGE NOISE

The task for this illustration is complicated because there are lamp posts in the picture that must be removed to allow the natural beauty of this scene to present itself. Detailed and exacting work such as this can be very time-consuming.

"... there are lamp posts in the picture that must be removed..."

STEP 1:
Open the image in Photoshop.

STEP 2:
Open the Layers pallet (Window>Layers palette).

REPLACING PEOPLE IN AN IMAGE

In this picture the bride was hopelessly obscured because the photographer's equipment literally fell apart and the film was ruined. The only way to fix the most precious shots was to substitute from other images. Here the bride was taken from another image and substituted to complete the shot. This is a drastic case, but often substitution of image elements from other shots is the easiest and best digital solution.

REMOVING SKIN PROBLEMS

A terrible bruise needed to be removed from this woman's face. There was not time to wait for her to heal and no current image that could be substituted. The solution was to repair the skin tone by selective work in the color channels. The goal was to maintain skin characteristic and facial shape while creating a more natural tone. Similar techniques can be used to remove birthmarks and other types of stains.

PUTTING LIFE INTO AN IMAGE

Sometimes putting the life back into an image is as easy as doing some color correction. In this case the dulled print was color corrected and life added to the image by working with highlights and changing some of the lighting effects. This pooch shows significant improvement. Similar techniques can help immeasurably with images that have aged, been poorly exposed, or which need a little change to make them dynamic.

REARRANGING ELEMENTS TO IMPROVE AN IMAGE

Sometimes everything you need for an image improvement is right in the photo you are fixing. In this case, the partial brick background was not the best setting for the subject. Using the beach from another part of the image helped add better character to the background. Often working with elements in the image you are correcting can provide the best results as there are fewer worries about matching film grain, colors, lighting configuration and tone.

Dramatic Changes in Setting

A more dramatic change in setting using a second background can make an enormous difference in the presentation of a subject. Here the racetrack is not quite so flattering to the subject as a colorful outdoor setting. In this case, few real alterations in lighting were necessary as the light in both images comes from the same direction. Adding the horse's drop shadow to the foreground helps complete the illusion.

DUOTONING IMAGES

Duotone works especially well with older images. Not only does the coloration seem to work well and imprint an appropriately aged look to images, but the multiple inks in printing actually help add a smoother print quality for press work. A popular effect is sepia toning. Here sepia tones are mimicked by CMYK process. Toning can prove effective in creating images for the web and negatives for printmaking as well.

ENHANCING IMAGE DETAILS

Adding a blue sky in place of the gray one above the building adds color and interest to this shot. The blue sets off and adds emphasis to the snow gathered in the eaves, along the roof and on the steeple. The addition also sets off the cross at the roof peak. The best thing about this technique is that it is one of the simplest things to do in Photoshop. All you do is make a selection and fill with a gradient of your choice.

GATHERING THE FAMILY

A technique unique to digital photography is the ability to combine images with some ease. In this project, it was impossible to get this whole family in the same place at the same time for a reunion picture, so the reunion was accomplished digitally. Most of the family was assembled for the first photo, and then the last brother was taken separately and added to the image. Similar lighting and setting make the images easy to combine.

RADII AND RESOLUTION:

The pixel radius is dependent on the image resolution. Scale filter effects depending on the DPI.

STEP 5 & 9:

STEP 11:

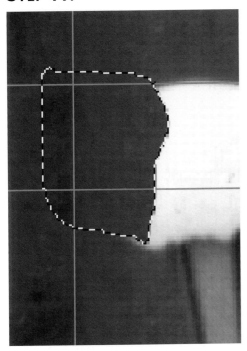

STEP 3:

Copy of the Background Layer by dragging it into the Duplicate Layer Icon at the bottom of the Layers palette.

STEP 4:

Zoom in to the lamp post in front of the door.

STEP 5:

Using the Marquee tool (with a feather radius of 10 pixels) select a rectangular area from the door's right side.

STEP 6:

Copy and Paste the selection to its own layer.

STEP 7:

Flip the layer horizontally (Edit>Transform>Flip Horizontal). Drag it to the other side of the door to cover a portion of the lamp post.

STEP 8:

Use the eraser tool to erase the parts of the pine tree which will also reveal part of the post you are illuminating.

STEP 9:

Move to the center part of the door and select a long, elliptical segment using the Lasso tool.

STEP 10:

Copy and Paste into its own layer, then drag over the lamp post. This covers most of the lamp post.

STEP 11:

Adjust the lamp post by using the Rubber Stamp tool on the Background Layer Copy. Remove snow from the lamp on the left to make the background column appear straight.

STEP 12:

Move to the next lamp post. Be careful not to obliterate the many lines on the brick wall behind the post.

STEP 13:

Bring a horizontal guide line to cross the top of the lamp-post, and vertically on the shadow area of the wall to the left of the post. Place another horizontal guide line on the lower part of the snow area.

STEP 14:

Double click the Lasso tool to get the Lasso Options, and select a Feather Radius of 5 pixels.

STEP 19:

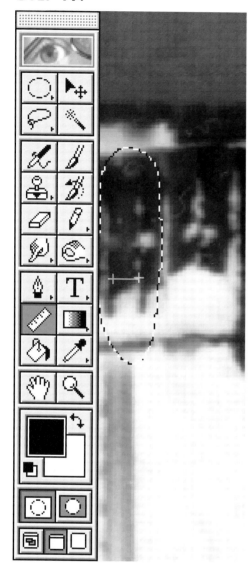

STEP 15:
Select a portion of the brick wall to be pasted over the snow on the top of the lamp.

STEP 16:
Press [Option/Alt]+[Command/Control]. While holding these, place the pointer in the middle of the selected area.

STEP 17:
Use the arrow to move the selected area over the snow, ensuring the brick lines are aligned. Continue holding the keys down while dropping and dragging over most of the snow-covered area. Work from both sides until an even appearance is obtained and the snow area is entirely covered. The up/down arrows can be used to adjust the placement of the selected sections and align the bricks.

STEP 18:
It is almost impossible to avoid an apparent pattern in the area. Use the Rubber Stamp tool to clean the patterns.

STEP 19:
Select the Magic Ruler. Measure the area between two regular fence rods.

STEP 20:
Click on the Lasso Tool and make a Selection.

STEP 21:
Deselect.

STEP 22:
Place your guides on the pillar to the left of the statue.

STEP 23:
Double-click the Rubber Stamp tool and set Opacity to 100% and Mode to Normal. Push the [Option/Alt] key and click on the left column at the point where the guides intersect.

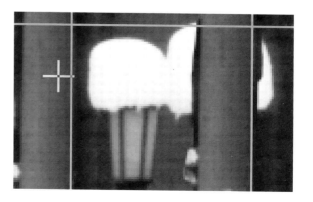

SNAP TO GRID LINES:

The Grid Lines will snap to, and you need to use care when working close to them as the brush will stick to the grid lines and interfere with your task completion.

STEP 29:

STEP 24:
Use the same technique with the Rubber Stamp Tool as was used on the wall to cover the post.

STEP 25:
Paint down until you run into the tree on the left column.

STEP 26:
Using the Lasso, select a small portion of brick wall to cover the top right hand snow area outside the column.

STEP 27:
While holding down the [Command/Option] keys on a Macintosh (or the [Control/Alt] keys on a PC) put your cursor in the center of the brick selection. Drag it to the part of the post to be covered. Drop the new brick into place.

STEP 28:
Now the base of the column is like the one behind the statue, except the column behind the statue is in a shadowed area. To borrow from the shadowed column, select the shadowed column using the Lasso.

STEP 29:
Copy and paste it.

STEP 30:
Press the "V" key to bring up the Move tool. Click on the pasted area and move it over to cover the lamp post, as well as to cover the base of the second lamp post.

STEP 31:
Press [Command/Control]+L, and use the middle Levels slider and the right slider to adjust the density of the brightness until it matches the lighting around it.

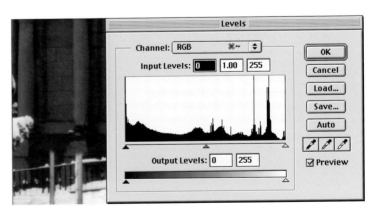

Step 35:

Step 32:

Using the Lasso, with a Feather Radius of 5 pixels, select areas to the right of each pole to complete the coverup.

Step 33:

Press [Command/Control]+H to hide the edges of the selection.

Step 34:

Use the Rubber Stamp tool to apply finishing touches.

Step 35:

The banister leading out of the picture in the bottom left corner needs to be removed. Do this simply by using the Lasso tool process once again to move a swatch of snow over it.

■ Adding Objects to Backgrounds

Our task for this image is to replace the sky, and make it a beautiful blue! We will also change the perspective of the buildings to straighten them up properly.

Step 1:

Select the sky (using the Magic Wand tool) while leaving the parts of the building intact. Also, be sure to leave an uneven white snow cap on the towers of the church.

Step 2:

Go to the Quick-Mask Mode. The building becomes overlaid with a mask that looks like a rubylith film.

"Our task for this image is to replace the sky, and make it a beautiful blue!"

STEP 3:

Use the Paint Brush tool to paint in the mask, toggling back and forth between the Paint Brush and the Eraser tool to add or remove those parts of the mask (red area) until the sky is isolated perfectly.

STEP 4:

With the selection is isolated, select the Linear Gradient tool and double-click to get the Linear Gradient Options dialogue box. Set the Foreground to Transparent in the pop-up menu. Make sure Transparency and Dither are checked, and Reverse is not checked. Set the Opacity at 100%.

STEP 4:

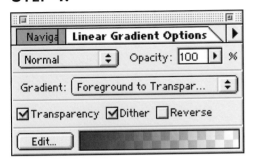

STEP 5:

Click on the Color Picker at the bottom of the tool box. Pick a deep blue color.

EXPERIMENT!

Be sure to take time to experiment with various tools and settings (such as color and gradient choices) to further your learning experience.

STEP 6:

Click-drag from the top of the sky down at an angle to the center of the church window to create a gradual gradient in the sky color. This fills the sky area with blue color.

STEP 6: AFTER

STEP 7:

Press the Space+[Command/Control]+ [Option/Alt] keys and click on the image.

STEP 8:

Show Rulers, then drag down a horizontal Guide Line.

STEP 9:

Place the guide line at the base of the building and notice that the perspective of the building is level.

Straighten the perspective of the building using the transform function and grids.

STEP 10:

Pull down two additional Guide Lines, placing one just above the doorway arch and the other approximately halfway up between the lower line and the top of the picture.

STEP 11:

Pull two vertical Guide Lines and place them approximately on both sides of the central portion of the building. This will help you see how "off kilter" the lines in the building are.

STEP 12:

Open Free Transform ([Command/Control] +T). A Bounding Box will appear around the entire image.

STEP 13:

Hold down the [Command/Control] key while dragging on corner anchors until the building lines are aligned with the Guide Lines. Press Enter when the goal is achieved.

STEP 14:

Using the Lasso tool, select the tip of the tower on the left.

STEP 15:

Copy and Paste into its own layer.

STEP 16:

Open the Move tool and move the tip of the tower into place on the top of the tower on the right.

STEP 17:

Fill in the sky area.

Persons missing from family photos like the one below can be added later with digital technology. The brother in Illustration P (below) will be added to Illustration Q (right).

P.

"... add the missing brother to the family portrait."

■ ADDING A PERSON TO THE PICTURE

The task for this image is to add a missing brother to the family portrait. Begin by opening the photos of the family, Illustration Q, and the missing brother, Illustration P.

Q.

STEP 1:
Drag the Background Layer to the New Layer Icon at the bottom of the Layers Palette.

STEP 2:
Drag the newly formed layer to the right 1.8" to add space to the left side of the photograph.

STEP 3:
Press [Command/Control]+E.

STEP 4:
Using the Lasso tool, select the lady to the left of the image, including rock.

STEP 5:
Add to your selection the entire left-hand part of the image from top to bottom (everything to the left of the lady).

STEP 6:
Name and save your selection. (Window>Show Channels> Select Menu>Save Selection) You could save this selection as "Background."

Step 7:

Go to the picture of the brother standing alone and copy this image. (Edit>Select All, press [Command/Control]+C)

Step 8:

Paste this image into the family group. (Edit>Paste Into) This process will Paste the brother into his own layer with a layer mask next to him.

Step 9:

Place cursor on the Ruler and Drag into photo to bring a grid down. Line this grid with the top of the tallest man's upper mid forehead.

Step 10:

Press [Command/Control] to create a Bounding Box around the brother. Since this brother's image is proportionally larger than the other subjects in the family picture, drag the cursor to one of the corner anchor points and drag the anchor point inward toward the center of the image until the brother's size is proportional to the size of the other subjects in the family photo. Line the grid with the top of the brother's forehead. Since the brother is wearing a hat, you will have to use your best judgement.

Step 11:

There is a line that exists between the two backgrounds that makes it obvious that the image has been retouched. Select the Eraser Tool with opacity set to 100. Select a large Soft Brush from the Brush Palette.

Step 12:

Making sure you are still on the background layer of the brother's portrait, begin erasing the background of this layer until the trees and foliage behind the subject appear to blend together and no evidence of the alteration is evident.

"... begin erasing the background until the trees and foliage appear to blend together..."

STEP 1:

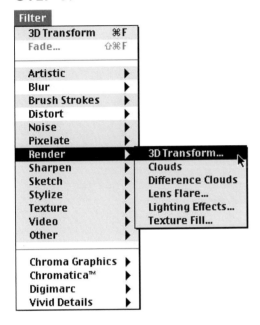

3-D TRANSFORMATION TOOL

To use the 3-D Transformation filter you must be in the RGB mode (Image > Mode> RGB>.

8. TABLETOP PHOTOGRAPH TECHNIQUES

Table Top Photography is basically used in advertising for catalogs. In the past photography was performed by very sophisticated and complicated camera equipment. Now it can be accomplished with a digital camera and computer.

■ 3-D TRANSFORMATION

Our task is to transform an image to a 3-D image. With the 3-D Transform Filter in Photoshop, an image perspective can be created in ways and with an ease never before possible.

STEP 1:

Open the image you want to transform, then (Filter> Render>3-D). A 3-D Transformation dialogue box will appear with a grayscale image of your original image.

STEP 2:

Select the Cube tool. This will produce a cursor in the form of a "+" with a white cube in the center.

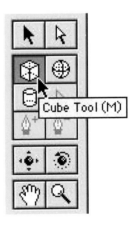

STEP 3:

Click on each of the six corners of the object to be transformed. This creates small red Anchor Points.

STEP 4:

Click on the Direct Selection tool (the white arrow), and go to the Anchor Point on the upper left side of the image and drag it to the next anchor point (located at the top corner of the left side of the front part of the box), and release the mouse button. This produces a red line between the two points.

STEP 4:

STEP 5:

Return to the first Anchor Point, click and drag downward in an arc fashion to the upper right hand corner Anchor Point. This creates a red outline of the top of the box.

STEP 6:

Return to the first Anchor Point and begin dragging downward and inward simultaneously. This will produce a green outline.

STEP 7:

Drag the green line down to the lower right hand corner of the box, producing a proportional outline of the entire box with the green line. This produces your selected cube.

STEP 8:

Go to the Options button in the dialogue box and click on it to produce the Options dialogue box.

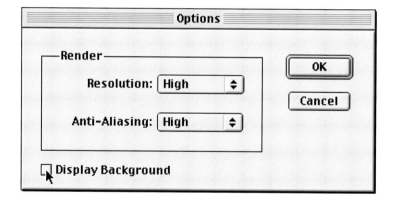

STEP 9:

In order to obtain a high quality output, it is important to select High in both the Resolution and Anti-Aliased areas. Also, make sure that the Display Background selection is not checked.

STEP 10:

In the 3-D Transformation dialogue box, choose the Field of View setting, and experiment with the settings.

STEP 11:

Click on the Dolly setting. This setting increases or decreases the size of the image while suspending it in space. Again, experiment to choose your settings.

STEP 12:

Move to the Trackball tool and click on it. This tool allows you to manipulate and change perspectives of the selected image, changing angles or rotating it. Play around with the Trackball to explore the nature of the settings.

"This tool allows you to manipulate and change perspectives..."

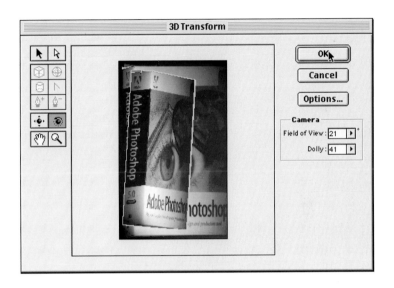

STEP 13:

Save the image by clicking on the OK button.

This illustration will be used to show Vignetting both to black and white.

R.

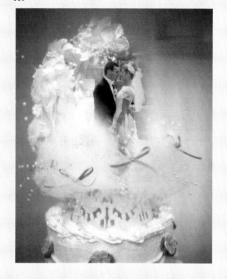

Remember, in this example we have only explored the rotation of a cube when we selected the Cube tool. You can produce other results using a cylinder or a sphere. Experiment and explore your possibilities.

■ VIGNETTING

Vignetting adds to an image by placing the focus of attention on the subject. A vignette can be any color you choose. Black and white are the colors more traditionally used in photography. This will be demonstrated using Illustration R.

STEP 1:

Double-click on the Elliptical Marquee tool. This produces a Marquee Options dialogue box. Set in 50 pixels in the Feather Option.

STEP 2:

Check the Anti-Aliased selection. Make sure to select Normal from the pull-down menu.

STEP 3:

Make the selection by choosing a starting point in the upper left corner. Pull the cursor down to the right until you have an elliptical area selected about the size that you desire. At this point, do not be concerned as to whether the selection is perfect.

"At this point, do not be concerned as to whether the selection is perfect."

STEP 6:

STEP 4:

Move the selection outline by placing the cursor into it and click-dragging the selection area.

STEP 5:

Invert the selection by pressing the [Command/Control]+ [Shift]+I keys down.

STEP 6:

Press the Delete Key. This will delete the unselected area, leaving you with a white vignette area.

STEP 7:

Select a color from the image by going to the Eyedropper tool and click on the desired color. Another option is to click on the Color Picker Foreground box to bring up the various color options. A color can be selected from the various colors available and used by holding down the [Option/Alt] key and pressing Delete.

After a color is selected for the background of the vignette, the results might look like this:

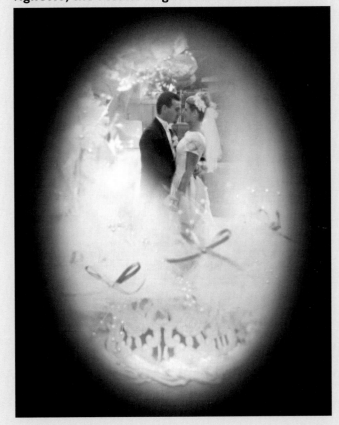

9. Managing Files & Final Output

After you have completed all of the desired retouching and/or restoration processes, you need to obtain the highest possible quality output for your finished product.

■ Output to Color Negative

In order to obtain a quality image in the final picture the negative must be created from a high resolution digital image. As an example, if you are planning on a Large-Format Print Reproduction (16 x 20 or larger), and your negative comes from 120-size film, the pixel resolution of the scan should be 4800 x 4800 for the image you will be working on. This image will require approximately 67 mb minimum to input into your computer. You should plan on needing three times that amount (Photoshop recommends a minimum of two times) to work on the image, or 201 mb of RAM, and approximately two times the amount to save the final image. While you can work on images with less RAM available, you will continue to experience frequent crashes.

The quality of pixel resolution, the type of scan, and the type of end product to be produced (either negative or print) depends on the size of print desired and the number of copies to be produced. However, Kodak has produced a chart that provides estimates for various types of outputs and film sizes. Please refer to this chart (page 107) that is being reproduced by permission of Kodak.

■ Output to Dye-Sublimation Printer

One of the major advantages of the dye-sub printer is that it provides a high quality print that color-matches in an almost perfect manner. In other words, the hues are more life-like, providing blacks that are black, a full scale of shades of gray, and colors that radiate a brilliance.

A dye-sub printer can print an image that is saved at 300 dpi in the RGB mode, and requires no additional special preparation.

■ Saving RAM (Purging the Clipboard)

There is nothing more frustrating than having a message pop up telling you there is "Insufficient Memory." Purging the Clipboard will free up room. This is an easy way to maintain usable RAM for the operation of Photoshop. Purging the History palette can free up room as well. A simple way to purge both at the same time is to go to Edit Menu>Purge>Purge All. When you receive the warning, consider it seriously before you click OK.

"... the negative must be created from a high resolution digital image."

10. PRINTERS

My concern in printing has always been threefold: quality color reproduction; photographic quality with longevity; and affordable price.

The type of printers we are considering in this chapter are computer-driven printers, regardless of size or cost. These issues will be addressed as we consider the various concerns in seeking the appropriate equipment to provide the output you desire and need to meet your customers' expectations.

> "My concern in printing has always been threefold..."

■ PRINT-OUT LONGEVITY

Longevity is the ability to print out a photographic quality print on a computer-driven printer that will last just as long as a normal color photograph.

When color photographs first came into existence, the color would begin to fade away in about 5 to 10 years. As film manufacturers worked to resolve this problem, they extended the life of color prints to 20 to 50 years. We now find history is repeating itself in digital photographic printing. When a digital photograph is printed on a photo-quality inkjet, the longevity of the print is about three years at best. This longevity is in incandescent lighting, and not direct sunlight. The problem lies in the type of inks available for the printer. Prints from Laser Printers last even less time. In contrast, dye-sub printers provide an output image that will last approximately 20 years.

While there is a current problem with longevity, a solution should be forthcoming in a short time. An alternate method of resolving the problem is to laminate the photograph with an ultra violet laminant. However, this requires an additional investment in laminating equipment. Because of the longevity issue, I do not deliver photographs to my customers that I have printed as a final product. However, because they are produced as photo quality prints, I do use them as proofs to obtain final approval before sending to a lab for processing.

The lab will produce a photographic print from your digital storage device that maintains photographic quality equal to a print made from a negative. Some lab printers are LED printers and can produce up to 20 x 30 prints from a 300 dpi digital image.

FUJIX Pictography 3000 and 4000 models are alternative printers produced by FUJI. The maximum size produced by a 3000 model is an 8.59 x 11.77 at 400 dpi resolution. This printer completes the task in a single-step operation that uses a laser diode exposure and thermal dye transfer using a three component color process: yellow, magenta and cyan. The 4000 uses a four-step printing process of photo-chemical and laser technologies that produces a photorealistic digital color print.

The maximum size of images for this model is approximately 12 x 18. The prints are guaranteed to last for fifty years.

It is important to check with your local lab to determine the type of service they offer for digital prints and the expected longevity.

■ Good Printers You Can Afford

There printers on the market today which provide you with "photographic quality" output, and Epson would seem to be the leader. There are other printer companies whose products produce a high quality product. Hewlett Packard, Cannon, and Apple are amongst the most familiar. Printers are usually rated by print quality in terms of resolution. The higher the dpi, the higher the resolution, and the finer the images appear.

■ Epson Printers

Let's first look at the Epson printers. Epson offers the following inkjet models as providing "photographic quality prints": the Stylus Color 600, the Stylus Photo 700, the Stylus Color 740, the Stylus Color 800, the Stylus Color 850, the Stylus Color 1520, the Stylus color 3000, and the Stylus Color EX. This is quite an array of selections, considering cost.

To begin with, "photo quality" does not necessarily equate to true photographic quality output. These printers may not produce the quality of photograph necessary for providing a finished product to your customer. They all, however, provide acceptable output for quality proofs. A rule of thumb: if you want a higher quality print, select a printer that uses six color ink cartridges rather than three in addition to the black cartridge. In the "reasonably priced" category, this would include the Stylus Photo 700 and the Stylus Photo EX.

While the selection is varied, and any of the listed printers may produce an adequate job for you, in addition to quality you must consider speed of output and print size desired. The Photo 700 will provide 8.5" x 44" outputs, while the Photo EX provides 11.7" x 44" output at the same resolution. The Color 1520 will produce variable sizes from 4" x 4" to 17" x 22", but does not provide 6 color Ink Jet printing. This is also true of the Color 3000, while both are billed as providing 1440 dpi photo quality color printing.

All of the photo quality Epson printers are capable of producing quality images. The primary problem is the longevity of these prints, which can only be increased by a laminating process.

"...'photo quality' does not necessarily equate to true photographic quality output."

■ HEWLETT PACKARD PRINTERS

Hewlett Packard is a well-known manufacturer of quality LaserJet printers. However, they do offer a couple of inkjet printers which provide photo quality output. These are the HP DeskJet 2000 Cse Professional Color Printer, HP DeskJet 1120 Cse model, the DeskJet 890 Cse Professional Color Printer, the DeskJet 697C Printer, the DeskJet 712C Photo-Color Printer, and the DeskJet 722C Printer. The 697C requires an additional upgrade cartridge to print photos (the HP Photo Cartridge). The remainder of the models are all affordable. However, they offer only 600 dpi with a special HP Photo REt II color dot enhancement that provides smaller color dots and finer images. They provide good proof photograph copies.

■ CANNON PRINTERS

Cannon offers three basic printers, all at reasonable prices. These models are the BJC-5000, the BJC-4400, and the BJC-250. The BJC-5000 boasts seven-color printing with 1440 x 720 dpi resolution, while the BJC-4400 model only prints at 720 x 360 dpi. The BJC-250 model is of doubtful quality for what a restoration artist desires in terms of output. The dpi of the other models is more consistent with a quality outcome. Both the 5000 and 4400 models would likely be good for proofing, and the 5000 model for potential final output.

■ DYE-SUB PRINTERS

KODAK and Fargo have been the primary developers and producers of the dye-sublimation printer, but these tend to be expensive (over $5,000). ALPS also produces dye-sub printers, and their printers tend to be available at a lower price than KODAK and Fargo. I have experience with the output of the ALPS-MD-1300 printer, which provides adequate quality output for black-and-white restored photographs and color prints smaller than 8 x 10. The problem is that, with color photos, it may produce lines from the various print head passes, and print quality can vary from ribbon to ribbon.

The value of using a dye-sub printer is that it has greater longevity as compared to inkjet printers. The dye-sub printer uses a color ribbon to produce the final product, and operates at a faster printing rate than inkjet printers, but slower than a laser printer.

This printer uses a process that involves the printing head heating the dyes, which then become gaseous (sublime) and penetrate the paper's special coating. The printer must have an additional "long-life ribbon" in place to ensure longevity of the color.

"The dye-sub printer uses a color ribbon to produce the final product..."

"... this printer would be a worthwhile investment in addition to an inkjet printer..."

This type of printer can be used to provide the customer a final printout of high quality (except for larger color prints) at this time. While other printers provide good proof pictures, the dye-sub printer produces true photo quality prints that will last at least 20 years. If you will be providing a number of final prints on an ongoing basis for your customers, this printer would be a worthwhile investment in addition to an inkjet printer to provide you with proofs.

■ Projects You Can Print at Home

If you own a dye-sub printer you can print anything within the capability of your printer for size outcome, with an 8 x 10 being the normal maximum size. The exception to this rule is that when you have an order for a large quantity of prints of the same image, it is better to have a negative produced and create the prints from this negative.

If you do not have a dye-sub printer, but the longevity problem is not an issue, you can print anything within the capacity of your printer. In any case, you can always produce proofs to show to your customer for final approval or to provide the lab for color matching purposes.

11. FILM RECORDERS

A Film Recorder is a device that creates a negative from your digital file. To obtain this service, you would normally seek out a color lab (now more commonly known as an "Imaging Lab") that has the capability to perform this task. An increasing number of labs are expanding their capability to provide this service, but the equipment is very expensive. Check with your lab to determine if they provide such a service, or to find out who does provide such a service.

■ REQUIREMENTS

What you choose for the final image output depends on the type of negative size you choose. If the customer wants the final print to be a smaller image size (up to 8 x 10), you can request a 35mm negative. This idea is to provide the quality product you desire and not overkill.

When your customer desires a large final print (16 x 20 or larger), a larger 4 x 5 negative must be obtained. The ideal format size is the 120 size negative. The larger negative formats are much more expensive than the smaller format. A 120 negative produces up to a 16 x 20 image. Services that provide this size are, however, difficult to find.

A transparency can also be processed at an Imaging Lab. To obtain a quality transparency, the finished digital image should be saved in a 4800 x 4800 dpi format.

■ COLOR MANAGEMENT SYSTEM PREFERENCES

Color management helps the consistent matching of the image colors seen on the screen to those that are output. A Color Management System (CMS) provides a more accurate representation of color consistency from one program or device to another. These devices and programs may individually vary in their ability to reproduce a full range of colors.

Photoshop 5.0 has a built-in color management system. The Photoshop color management system is based on the International Color Consortium (ICC) standard for cross-application. The Photoshop Color Management Module (CMM) that allow the user to plug into ICC processes is an adjustable module that aligns with other color matching applications. Photoshop has a built-in CMM that can be changed to match the settings of another application. The computer operating system also specifies a CMM. In the Macintosh, the CMM is located in Apple ColorSync (2.5 or later). In the PC, the CMM is located in the Microsoft ICM 2.0. (Refer to page 81 of the Photoshop 5.0 User's Manual).

Color preference can be set up to match the demands of whatever printing device you are using. Again, the procedures are found in

> "A transparency can also be processed at an Imaging Lab."

"Color corrections can be fine-tuned more fully with color correction software."

the User's Manual and need not be duplicated here. Just a reminder: it is always important to calibrate your monitor after installing Photoshop and before you use the program. This is normally a one-time process unless you reinstall the Photoshop program. The procedures for accomplishing this task begin on page 82 of the User's Manual.

Color corrections can be fine-tuned more fully with color correction software. As an example, Pantone Color Correction is suggested for use with windows. My experience is that the Macintosh ColorSync is highly effective in providing consistent output if set up to match the printing device. With Windows-based computers, the users I have worked with have had difficulty matching color output to on-screen colors.

The Adobe Gamma Module is a walk-through program that Adobe 5.0 has developed to assist you in walking through the process of setting up the CMS. If you use this process, it will walk you through the process step-by-step, question by question until the system is set up specifically for your system. This is a one-time process unless you reinstall Photoshop for some reason.

12. DEVELOPING YOUR MARKET

■ SELLING YOURSELF AND YOUR WORK

This chapter is designed primarily for those individuals who are seeking to establish a digital photo retouching business from scratch. The principles could also be applied by photographers who want to expand their business to include digital retouching.

The most important element in any privately owned business is the marketing of your services. You can never relax your efforts if you are to be successful: always keep an eye open for opportunities to sell yourself and your services and to make prospective contacts. Normal business processes are important: you must have business cards; advertise in various media (depending upon your available financial resources); establish a consistent telephone number and address, and open a business bank account. Don't forget your business and resale licenses. After that, you'll need to look at a plan for developing your market.

■ THE THREE-POINT MARKETING PLAN

The Three-Point Marketing Plan provides you with a structured manner of developing your digital retouching service. To begin with, you are in the market to retouch photographs, so obviously photographers are the most likely to become your focus to begin developing your business.

■ INITIATING CONTACT

Begin this phase of the process by identifying the professional photographers in your area. Go to the Yellow Pages in your local telephone directory. Begin with those in your geographic vicinity, and determine the limits of your contact by how far you are willing to travel. Contact every photo studio and commercial photographer within your predetermined driving distance. Make telephone calls, perhaps as many as 100 at a sitting. Think of this process as entertainment; be positive and keep going until you reach your calling number goal or you run out of energy.

When you make contact, have your approach to each new prospect pre-planned. Explain that you have been trained as a digital retoucher and restoration artist using Photoshop. Good digital retouchers are very hard to find, whereas bad ones are common. Offer to send them some literature describing your work and your price list. Take notes as to the name of the photo studio and the individual you talked to, recording any personal or specific information that might have been shared.

> "When you make contact, have your approach to each new prospect pre-planned."

"Talk to the owner/power person if possible."

When you are making the initial contact, you may encounter a receptionist who tries to keep you from the decision-maker. It is important to treat this person with respect, and gather important information in order to determine who is the "power person" for the business. Explain to them you are a professional photo retoucher, and that the owner/photographer always has need for such services. Keep a positive perspective, reframing any negative responses as positives. Remember, if you visit the studio, the person you are talking to will likely also be the first person you encounter when you walk in the door. Don't make assumptions about who may answer the telephone – it may be the owner, or one of the owner's family members. Talk to the owner/power person if possible. Make certain you have the correct, complete address for the studio.

■ Communicating As A Follow-up

If you promise to send material, be sure you do within a week from the time you called. Develop an introductory cover letter, describing the services you have to offer. Also include with the letter a current price list (see Developing Your Price List), a copy of your brochure (see Developing a Marketing Brochure), and a coupon for one-half hour of free retouching. When doing mailings, it is handy to have a computer and mail-merge capability to address the letters and envelopes, and personalize the letter with the date of the phone call and the name of the person you spoke with.

■ Completing the Follow-up Visit

The follow-up visit should be planned within a month or two, and no more than six months, after you send out the follow-up information. Plan out your visits by mapping out the location of all studios you have contacted and need to visit. Make the most effective use of your time. Once your visiting plan is formulated, call each studio to make an appointment. Plan your visits for approximately ten minutes and maintain the plan unless invited to stay longer. It is important that you demonstrate respect for the photographer's time. Bring samples of your work with you, discuss their business needs, and review your price list. Assure them of your policies before beginning a job.

Keep the interview on a positive note, regardless of the demeanor of the photographer. If you alienate one photographer, you could easily find yourself "blackballed." If you follow this Three-Point Marketing Plan, you will soon find your business growing. Pursue this plan until all the identified potential customers in your area have been contacted.

■ Sell Your Work

Consider every person you meet a potential customer. This means taking the opportunity to share your business with them. If such an opening does not present itself, treat them with respect and maintain a positive contact with them. Even if you never see them again, you never know who is observing you.

Be positive and enthusiastic about what you do as well as who you are. There is nothing more catching than a smile. When you feel comfortable, join the local photographer's association and present yourself and your work there. Join networking groups and arrange to provide presentations to the various community organizations in your area. If you are having difficulty identifying these organizations, contact your local chamber of commerce and they will gladly provide you with a list for a small fee.

Keep in mind that the possibilities are limitless! You are only limited by your own imagination and any unwillingness to venture forth into the unknown to explore new territory. The more fearless you can allow yourself to be, the more effectively you can sell your services.

■ Where Are Your Markets?

There is more than enough work available for competent digital retouchers. Once you complete the Three-Point Marketing Plan, do not sit back and wait for the work to pour in, no matter how successful your response appeared. The effective service provider must always be selling and seeking new markets.

There is no reason to spend your time or energy visiting the chain photo shops, usually found in shopping malls. They usually sell package deals for a minimum fee and either avoid retouching or complete their own. One hour photo studios are also unproductive marketing targets. Some of the potential markets you can explore are portrait, commercial and animal photographers.

■ Portrait Photographers

These photographers specialize in portraits of individuals and families, and are involved in various types of portraiture. Jobs from them may be simple touch-ups or may involve more complicated processes such as adding body parts or moving family members in a portrait. These professionals may become a rich referral source, as many individuals bring old family photographs needing repair to photographers. It is important for you to constantly remind them of the types of work you can accomplish.

COPYRIGHT & PERMISSIONS

As your business expands and your work becomes known, it is not unusual for you to be approached by individuals who would like for you to "work your magic" with their family portraits. Remember that the professional photographer who created the original portrait hold the copyright, which is effective for 50 years. If a professional photographer is involved, it is important to work with or through the photographer and not with his or her customer. If the photographer does not want to be involved in the process, be sure to obtain the photographer's permission to alter the photograph. In such a case it would be appropriate to receive a signed release. Once again, it is important to contact the photographer for permission. This will not only keep your legal liability clear, but it may provide you with a positive contact (you have demonstrated your respect for the photographer's professional standing!) and open the door for future work with that photographer.

"Most ad agencies complete their own photo manipulations in-house."

■ Commercial Photographers

If you do not have personal connections with an advertising agency, it is fruitless to attempt to make a marketing contact. Most ad agencies complete their own photo manipulations in-house. These are usually very closed systems. However, commercial photographers work with ad agencies directly. If you are fortunate enough to work with a commercial photographer, and he or she is impressed with your work, this might provide an opening into an entirely new marketing area for you.

■ Animal Photographers

Both horse and dog photographers occasionally need an expert photo artist. Contact local breeding and show ranches and dog show breeders to inquire as to who the local photographers are who work with their animals.

■ Photo Restoration and the Yellow Pages

You may generate some business directly by running a small, one-line ad in the Yellow Pages under Photo Restoration. Always include your name and telephone number.

■ Developing a Marketing Brochure

When developing a marketing brochure, sell the potential customer on your skill. If you are just starting out with limited funds, you probably cannot afford the expense of hiring a graphics designer to develop an expensive brochure for you. So, develop one for yourself. Keep the following in mind:

1) **Who is your prospective customer base? Will they be more responsive to something that is "wild and crazy" or to a more conservative approach?**

2) **What example do you have available that might best reach out and "grab" them, and yet demonstrate your expert ability?**

3) **Keep it simple, but creative. Use gray-scale, and print it out on a LaserJet printer if possible.**

4) **Include a return address.**

■ What Will a Newsletter do for You?

A newsletter can serve as an effective communication tool and personal link between you and photographers. Allow your creativity to flow freely as you develop a newsletter - you want it to capture attention. The goal is for anyone reading the newsletter to equate you with retouching. There are a number of specifics to include in a newsletter:

- **Provide samples of your work**
- **Provide a copy of your price list**
- **Share triumphs and failures**
- **Inject humor whenever possible**
- **Explain the benefits of doing business with your service**

If you have trouble writing effectively and/or creatively, seek the help of a friend. Match graphics to your stories, which you can create out of your life events.

If you can be persistent in producing your newsletter and get it out on a regular basis, you may discover long-term benefits accruing. Send your newsletters to your regular mailing list, and carry extra copies with you to hand out to potential customers.

■ Developing a Price List

It is important to develop a realistic price list that will provide for your business needs, yet provide your potential customers with a cost incentive over what they would pay at a lab. It is important to indicate an hourly rate, but develop a specific task price list. Humor may help customer resistance a little. Some examples of specific tasks that I include on my price list are:

- **Open Eyes**
- **Head Replacement**
- **Changing Hairstyle**
- **Changing Backgrounds**
- **Ear Straightening**
- **Animal Leg Placement Changes**
- **Animal Gender Alterations**
- **Digital 8 x 10 Prints**
- **Convert an Image to a Negative**

"... you may discover long-term benefits accruing."

APPENDIX A

■ SUGGESTED SOFTWARE PLUG-INS

Plug-ins are extensions that are installed into Photoshop to add utility. They are designed to enhance and expedite Photoshop functions. There are several well known products on the market.

■ EXTENSIS

Intellihance 2.0. Intellihance is a tool that optimizes photo images in a single step. This is accomplished by applying filters for contrast, brightness, saturation, sharpness, and despeckle. The manner in which filters are applied can be customized by choosing from pre-defined menus or using the Fine Tune option for user control. Preference can be saved and applied to multiple images.

Mask Pro. Mask Pro quickly creates professional quality masks. This tool averages out a color sample, keeping or dropping colors that have been selected, until only the desired image remains. The program accurately removes all but the image that is desired to be saved, leaving the image smooth and free of jagged edges. The edges are softened, and the image is ready to be used.

■ CHROMA GRAPHICS

Edge Wizard. This tool lets the user make smooth, natural-looking edges for superior compositing and retouching results. A variety of edging selections are available, depending on the need: Quick Edge allows the choice of the direction to blend the edge instead of feathering; Gaussian Edge prevents halos by allowing blending and dithering; Variable Color Edge uses color range analysis of the image to determine the best possible edge; and Edge Brush allows the user to draw different edge types.

Magic Mask. Magic Mask simplifies editing tasks. A number of options are available. The Color Brush allows selection of multiple objects with independent color ranges simultaneously; the Magic Lasso automatically finds the edges of an object with "snap-to-edge" technology to provide sharp cutouts; the Nudge tool provides quick fine-tuning to directly manipulate any selection by nudging; and the Density Mask creates smooth color corrections with appropriate gradient changes at any degree of saturation.

Chromatica. The Chromatica tool allows any object to be selected instantly. Simply drag the ChromaMask tool over the object, and the object is immediately selected instead of having to use the Magic Wand and Lasso tools. Objects can also be recolored while keeping all of the detail and nuance of the original image. Choose the desired color, and the new colors to match the originally selected color are automatically calculated. It is important to go through the tutorial before using this program.

■ TEST STRIP

Test Strip is one of the best products available at this time to assist in adjusting the color balance of your image, and it is very simple to use. This is a powerful color correction tool which makes proofing easier, faster, and more precise. It provides a shortcut to achieve accurate color reproduction while eliminating the need for multiple color proofs. Test Strip offers full-screen previews, zooming, a Before and After comparison, precise changes, a Task List, and Test Proofs.

Maximum Size Prints from Various Digital Files

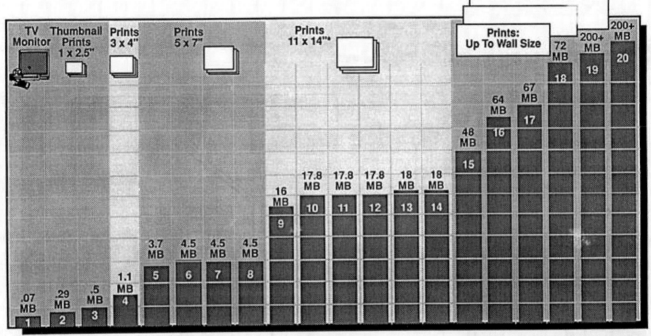

1. Photo CD @ Base/16
2. Photo CD @ Base/4
3. DC 20
4. DC 50, Photo CD @ Base

5. EOS·3 (CANON)
6. DCS 410 & 420 (NIKON)
7. EOS·5 (CANON)
8. Photo CD @ 4 Base

9. Drum Scan 135 Film
10. EOS·1 (CANON)
11. DCS 460 (CANON)
12. DCS 465 (120-size back)
13. RFS 3570 & 2035 Film Scanners
14. Photo CD @ 16 Base

15. 120 Film, 6 x 6 cm on Pro Photo CD @ 64 Base
16. 4 x 5" Film on Pro Photo CD @ 64 Base
17. Drum Scan 120 Film
18. 120 Film, 6 x 9 cm on Pro Photo CD @ 64 Base
19. Drum Scan 4 x 5" Film
20. Drum Scan 8 x 10" Film

* 11 x 14s are possible via skilled lab technician.

Take Pictures. Further.™ In The Portrait Market.

Appendix C

■ Glossary of Terms

anti-aliasing — a process that smooths the rough edges (or jaggies) of bitmapped graphics. This is normally accomplished by blurring the edges.

bit — the smallest piece of computer information. The computer is a binary device that uses binary numbers (0 or 1). This term is also used with color to describe the basic units of each of the RGB colors used by the computer. Example: a 24-bit color would indicate that there are 8-bits (basic units) of color information available for each of the RGB colors.

bitmap — an image that is made up of a cluster of dots (or pixels).

burn — a darkroom term used to describe the selective darkening of an image.

byte — eight bits. May also refer to a character on the screen.

clicking — pressing and immediately releasing the mouse button. When you click on something, you position the cursor pointer over it and then click.

contrast — the relationship between dark and light areas in a photograph. Contrast can be either high or low. High contrast occurs when sharp tones shift from dark to light with few middle tones. Low contrast exists when the image includes many middle tones.

cropping — providing emphasis on the subject of the photo by trimming. Only a portion of the original photograph is used.

despeckle — a filter that removes grain from an image.

distorting — changing the appearance of an image by deforming or contorting the whole picture or part of the image away from its natural appearance.

dodge — this is a darkroom term used to describe selective lightening of an image.

dpi — dots per inch. A term that measures the resolution of a printer, scanner, or monitor by referring to the number of dots in a one-inch line. This process defines how many dots of information a device can resolve in input or output. The more dots per inch, the higher the resolution.

drag — moving the cursor while holding down the mouse button. This may be a way of moving an object, selecting an area, or moving down a menu.

feather — gradually blending an image by softening the edge.

file formats — the structure in which the data for a particular document is stored. In Photoshop there are ten different formats.

TIFF (Tagged Image File Format) — this has become the primary standard format that allows users to cross platform limitations. Most other computers can open an image saved in TIFF format. TIFF permits compression without loss of image quality.

EPS (Encapsulated PostScript) — the EPS format provides a high-resolution image that may be required by some page layout programs for separations.

JPEG (Joint Photographics Experts Group) — A compression format which tosses out redundant information. Data is lost. Compression can be conducted at a low level (minimal loss of data), but the higher the compression ratio the greater the loss of data, degrading the quality of the image. This format is not normally effective for creating photographic quality prints since once the data is lost, it cannot be recovered.

gigabyte — a measure of computer memory or disk space that's equal to 1,024 megabytes or 1,073,741,824 bytes. It is abbreviated as G, GB, or gig.

grayscale — in photographic terms, a picture that contains shades of gray as well as black and white.

halftone — a method of converting an image into a pattern of small dots. The pattern of dots is described by a "line screen" with higher numbered screens resulting in better looking photos.

jaggies — the blocky, stair-stepped look common to low resolution bitmapped graphics.

kilobyte — a measure of computer memory or disk space or document size that is equal to 1,024 bytes. It is abbreviated as K.

layers — *a means of separating the parts of an image, or layering. A specific layer can be adjusted or deleted without impacting on any other layer.*

marquee — *the series of moving dots that surround a selected area.*

megabyte — *a measure of computer memory or disk space or application size that's equal to 1,024 K, or 1,048,576 bytes. It is abbreviated as MB, mb or meg.*

noise — *a special effect provided by a software filter that adds photo paper grain or other speckled effects. Resembles the noise seen on a television set.*

palette — *a floating window within an application that is normally located above an open document, permitting easy access to its contents.*

pixel — *the smallest element of a picture that can be controlled by the computer. The plural, pixels, is often used to describe the total number of dots that make up the entire image. Pixel is short for picture element (pix-el), and is often called dots.*

ppi (pixels per inch) — *the number of pixels per inch in an image. This concept is often used interchangeably with dpi.*

resolution — *the density of pixels in an image.*

saturation — *a description of how pure a color is; the richness and brightness of a color.*

shadow — *the darkest part of a photograph.*

sharpness — *the crispness of the appearance of the image.*

shift-click — *to hold down the [Shift] key while clicking the mouse button. The process of shift-clicking permits the selection of multiple objects.*

Index

Other Books from
Amherst Media, Inc.

Infrared Photography Handbook

Laurie White

Covers b&w infrared photography: focus, lenses, film loading, film speed rating, heat sensitivity, batch testing, paper stocks, and filters. Photos illustrate IR film in portrait, landscape, and architectural photo-graphy. $29.95 list, 8½x11, 104p, 50 b&w photos, charts & diagrams, order no. 1419.

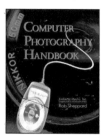

Computer Photography Handbook

Rob Sheppard

Learn to make the most of your photographs using computer technology! From creating images with digital cameras, to scanning prints and negatives, to manipulating images, you'll learn all the basics of digital imaging. $29.95 list, 8½x11, 128p, 150+ photos, index, order no. 1560.

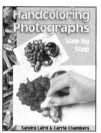

Handcoloring Photographs Step-by-Step

Sandra Laird & Carey Chambers

Learn to handcolor photographs step-by-step with the new standard in handcoloring reference books. Covers a variety of coloring media and techniques with plenty of colorful photographic examples. $29.95 list, 8½x11, 112p, 100+ color and b&w photos, order no. 1543.

The Art of Portrait Photography

Michael Grecco

Michael Grecco reveals the secrets behind his dramatic portraits which have appeared in magazines such as *Rolling Stone* and *Enter-tainment Weekly*. Includes: lighting, posing, creative development, and more! $29.95 list, 8½x11, 128p, order no. 1651.

Photographer's Guide to Polaroid Transfer

Christopher Grey

Step-by-step instructions make it easy to master Polaroid transfer and emulsion lift-off and add new dimensions to your photographic imaging. Fully illustrated every step of the way to ensure good results the very first time! $29.95 list, 8½x11, 128p, order no. 1653.

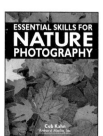

Essential Skills for Nature Photography

Cub Kahn

Learn all the skills you need to capture landscapes, animals, flowers and the entire natural world on film. Includes: selecting equipment, choosing locations, evaluating compositions, filters, and much more! $29.95 list, 8½x11, 128p, order no. 1652.

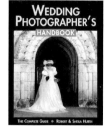

Wedding Photographer's Handbook

Robert and Sheila Hurth

A complete step-by-step guide to succeeding in the worl of wedding photography. Packed with shooting tip equipment lists, must-get photo lists, business strategie and much more! $24.95 list, 8½x11, 176p, index, b& and color photos, diagrams, order no. 1485.

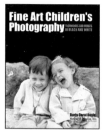

Fine Art Children's Photography

Doris Carol Doyle

Learn to create fine art portraits of children in black white. Included is information on: posing, lighting f studio portraits, shooting on location, clothing selectio working with kids and parents, and much more! $29.9 list, 8½x11, 128p, order no. 1668.

Special Effects Photography Handbook

Elinor Stecker Orel

Create magic on film with special effects! Little or n additional equipment required, use things you probabl have around the house. Step-by-step instructions guid you through each effect. $29.95 list, 8½x11, 112p, 80 color and b&w photos, index, glossary, order no. 1614.